Old Pakefield and Kirkley

Elizabeth Freeman and Jason Freeman

Strolling along the prom in front of the Victoria Hotel. Walter and Amy Freeman "bowling along the promenade" with their first baby in the 1920s.

Stenlake Publishing Ltd

© 2015 Elizabeth Freeman and Jason Freeman
First Published in the United Kingdom, 2015
Stenlake Publishing Limited
54-58 Mill Square, Catrine, KA5 6RD
www.stenlake.co.uk

ISBN 978-1-84033-699-3

Printed by
Blissetts, E1 – 8 Shield Drive,
West Cross Industrial Park, Brentford, TW8 9EX

ACKNOWLEDGEMENTS

Our thanks to:-
The staff of the Lowestoft Record Office for their kind assistance at all times, and for allowing us to use the following photographs from their archives:-

Pg 4   view from Pakefield church tower - LRO1300/85/74
Pg 13   Pakefield Street & Ship Inn - LRO 1300/85/115
Pg 17   Cunningham School children LRO 1300/85/124
Pg 21   Entrance to Lake Lothing - LRO 1300/72/2/2
Pg 23   looking up Pakefield Street near Ship Inn - LRO1300/85/113
Pg 32   Kirklwy water tower - LRO 1300/69/302
Pg 62   Cliff House [pre Grand Hotel] - LRO 1300/69/203
Pg 72   Firs Hotel - LRO1300/85/118

Billy Keith for lifeboat information.
Stuart Jones of the Port of Lowestoft Research Society, for the use of the following photographs:-
Pg 26 Pakefield lifeboat - courtesy of Port of Lowestoft Research Soc
Pg 28 James Leath lifeboat - courtesy of Port of Lowestoft Research Soc
Pg 28 Hugh Taylor lifeboat - courtesy of Port of Lowestoft Research Soc

The following people for their generosity in lending photos from their collections:-
Joseph Beckett, Rosemary Pye, Paul Durbidge, Avery and Arthur Bailey, Robert Porter, Mike Utton, Roy Scarlet, Phillip Rasberry, Paul Meadez, Dr Peter Baker
Canon Bob Baker, vicar of Pakefield church, for his kind assistance whilst researching parish records.

Jim Coyle and Victor Bristol, staff of the British Newspaper Library, whose consistent patience and help over several years is greatly appreciated.

A special thanks to Eline Freeman for being tolerant, as she watched piles of research gradually take over the house, and for living with the hope that one day, soon, it would all be over and life could be minimal again.

We wish to particularly thank Richard Stenlake, and his team, for publishing this book, and for saying, "Stop, you've done enough," and for his patience waiting for the day when we actually handed it over to him.

For staff in the following archives where we needed to research:-
Lowestoft Record Office; Ipswich Record Office; Lowestoft Maritime Museum; Lowestoft Museum Oulton Broad; Norwich Record Office; National Archives, Kew; National Maritime Museum, Greenwich; London Metropolitan Archives; Guildhall Library, London; Imperial War Museum, London; British Library, London; British Newspaper Library, London; Women's Library LSE, London.

Introduction

The ancient parishes of Pakefield and Kirkley in north east Suffolk are part of the Anglo Saxon hundred of Mutford and lie between Lake Lothing to the north and Kessingland (a significant Anglo-Saxon and medieval port) to the south. To the west of Pakefield was a swathe of rough pasture known as Runnel Heath where Pontins Holiday Camp and the Pakefield Pet Hotel now stand. Kirkley on the west is bounded by the Fen – a stream flowing down to Kirkley Hamm on Lake Lothing, from Bloodmoor Hill. The boundary between runs down Pakefield Street and Stradbrook Road and the people of Pakefield and Kirkley were neighbours. Pakefield Street – where the fisherfolk, blacksmith, shopkeepers and clothesmakers of both villages lived – was described in 1861 by a visitor as "little more than a collection of fishermen's cottages abutting on a sand cliff." There were a few farms with most of the parish land used for agriculture, but life was largely focused on the sea. The Pakefield Beach Company was formed around 1800; its Roaring Boys worked not just in fishing, but also helped ships in distress, and manned the two Pakefield lifeboats. The decades around 1800 marked some major changes to the parishes, with the enclosure of all the commons and the arrival of the Turnpike London Road in the 1790s. The Tithe Maps of the 1840s record patterns of settlement that had persisted for probably hundreds of years (perhaps going back to Domesday itself), but this was on the eve of huge changes.

With Peto's development of Lowestoft in the 1860s, Kirkley sea front became the pleasure quarter of Sir Samuel Morton Peto's new town of Lowestoft, and the railway began to bring thousands of people from all over England seeking new opportunities in building, tourism and the industries that supported the burgeoning fishing fleet. Landowners and entrepreneurs dreamt of marine mansions lining the sea shore, and investors from London purchased plots to develop great housing estates between the London Road and the cliff top. The villages flourished -with one hotel, the Empire, described as the most luxurious on the east coast. However it was not to last. The sea, ever giving and taking along the sandy shoreline, began to attack the sea wall with which Peto had encased the Kirkley cliff. Lowestoft Corporation, in what turned out to be a very successful effort to stop this incursion, threw out groynes and breakwaters all the way down to the edge of the town boundary at Pakefield Street, but this proved disastrous for the village of Pakefield. The sea on the east coast tends to scour southward of any promontory, and the final southernmost groyne caused it to bite deeply into the Pakefield cliffs, destroying the attempts at sea defence of the local landowners, and eroding hundreds of feet of land. Whole streets, newly laid out and built, were obliterated, along with the most ancient dwellings of Pakefield Street. Pakefield Church, once over a mile from the sea, came within a stone's throw of the waves; even part of the graveyard was taken.

The 20th century was, for Pakefield, almost its last. The destruction wrought by the sea was accompanied by the uncertainty, devastation and death of two world wars, during both of which Lowestoft and its surroundings were very much on the front line. Kirkley suffered bombardment and bombing during the First World War, while the men from both villages faced the silent menace of mines and U-boat attack while out at sea. During the Second World War, Lowestoft, fortified as it was to deter seaborne invasion, and with its naval bases focused on the harbour, was one of the most heavily bombed parts of the UK. Pakefield shared in the battle -its shoreline was dotted with guns and radar stations, barbed wire and mines covered the beach, and fishermen needed permission to put to sea. The darkest day was when incendiary bombs completely gutted the ancient parish church.

The coastal erosion brought Pakefield to its knees, and most of the parish was incorporated into Lowestoft. This was however, its physical salvation, as Sydney Mobbs, the Lowestoft Borough Surveyor was an expert in sea defence construction. Throughout the 1930s and into the 1940s, a vast concrete sea wall, topped with a promenade, together with an extensive system of breakwaters, was constructed to encase the cliffs. The wall's foundations went deep to prevent undermining, and the cliffs themselves were strengthened with concrete. Finally the erosion slowed, and then stopped. With the conclusion of the Second World War, Pakefield found safety once more, not only from air raid and combat, but from the sea's onslaught too.

Since the 1940s, Pakefield and Kirkley have continued to develop, and many have found peace and happiness enjoying the bracing sea air. The culture of both places has changed immeasurably since Peto first marked out his development plots – there are no beach companies, the fishing has all but ended, the ship building industry replaced with supermarkets.

The authors' connection with Pakefield goes back to the early 1500s, when their ancestor William Colby moved to the village, so beginning a dynasty of fishing folk whose destinies were bound up with that of both parishes.

Pakefield started out as the estate of an early Anglo-Saxon farmer called Pagga. Whose farm was probably near the site of the church. The houses and barn in this picture belonged to the rector, being some of the lands from which he gained his living, together with a right to tithes and half a dole of herring or mackerel from each fishing boat of the parish. The house nearest the church was his parsonage from the 1600s until around 1800. The track, now called the Causeway (from "Corseway"), was formerly known as the Bierway, both words referring to its role as the last journey for the dead of the village.

Houses clustered around the church and the Green (which is now the church car park – seen in the foreground here), but there were also outlying farms. In the time of Domesday Book, there were three main landowners – the King, Earl Hugh and the Manor of Mutford – each of whom had freemen under them who lived in the village and farmed the land. In total there were ten free families in Pakefield. The Manor of Mutford continued to hold land in Pakefield until the 1840s – a relic of an ancient Saxon administration system probably from the 8th century when the chief settlement in each hundred held lands throughout the hundred. The white houses in this picture were old. Pottery from the site shows there was occupation at least from the 1500s. The car park was a common until 1799, when it was "enclosed" and assigned to the rector. The church and these cottages had been far from the sea, but erosion made it look as if the whole lot would go over the cliff. Finally massive sea defences (seen under construction here), built in the 1930s, saved this area from destruction.

The houses, in what was Church Lane, (later Church Street, then St. Margaret's Road, now Saxon Road) – seen in front of the church in this picture – are likely to occupy the sites of medieval tenements, although the current houses seem to be early 19th century. In 1841 they were nearly all occupied by agricultural labourers – families like the Seeleys, Knights and Ravens.

These cottages were at the very far end of Church Lane, nearest to the sea and were built on a plot of land owned in 1841 by John Davie and occupied by Robert Raven, an agricultural labourer and his family. With the encroachment of the sea, they were pulled down sometime in the 1930s and replaced by a public convenience.

There were cottages both sides of Church lane, which ran from Mill Common (roughly where the Seventh Day Adventist Church is now) to the church. The three cottages on the left were Nos. 2, 4 and 6 St. Margarets Road. They were built before 1833 on land that had been the site of a single dwelling since at least the 1600s. They were purchased by Rev. Hunt in 1936 for £125 to augment the churchyard. Given the pace of erosion that had been taking place, the owners may have been relieved to sell. Today you can see where the tenement was by the different ground levels in the churchyard.

Towards the south of the parish was the manor of Rothenhall, centred on what became Pakefield Hall Farm. Probably this was a desirable location because there is a spring. It was occupied in Roman times, with trading links to the continent. At the time of Domesday, there were two freemen, who each had fairly large estates (30 and 40 acres), farmed by tenant farmers, with woodland for pigs. One of the estates paid nine shillings and 600 herrings, indicating that fishing was taking place. There was a moated manor house here in the 16th century, of which only part of the moat survives today, the rest of the buildings being either modern or old farm buildings. This is an area of truly ancient vintage. For many years, people have found old coins in the cliff falls, but beneath the cliff, there was a prehistoric forest, from which remains of elephants, bears, elk and rhinoceros have been recovered. Around the turn of the millennium, Paul Durbidge and his colleague Bob Mutch hit the headlines when they found worked flints in situ, undisturbed in the clay, together with mammal bones of animals that are extinct. It was evidence of people living in Pakefield from 700,000 BC. The microscopic mammal bones, animal teeth, and most importantly of all, a very rare extinct water vole, gave evidence of the age of the period.

Pakefield Church is actually two churches – one dedicated to St. Margaret and the other to All Saints. The two parts were established by the different manors of the parish – one located near the church, known in the middle ages as "Pakefield Pyes", or "Drayton" (after the families that owned it in the 14th century), and the other located in the ancient village of Rothenhall. It is possible that each chose to build here because this was consecrated land, and the site may have had some pre-Christian significance due to the large sarcen stone which today rests under the church tower. The lords of these manors had the right to appoint a rector to each "mediety" of the church, and they were unwilling to give this up, so for much of its history, these were two, separate, churches.

The shape of the church owes a great deal to the work of Richard Graunt, who was the first to hold both medieties, in the 15th century. He carried out much structural work, including building the tower, lengthening the chancel, inserting new windows, and placing a crypt or charnel house beneath the altar of the southern mediety. This picture is taken from the short lived Lorna Grove, which ran from the end of Church Road (now All Saints Road) to the Cliftonville Estate, along the cliff top.

LOWESTOFT. THE FONT, PAKEFIELD CHURCH. 39.

Pakefield Church has a number of medieval features, such as this font, carved in the late 1300s or early 1400s. It depicts a hart with crown, lions and angels. The "rich hart" may symbolise Richard II, but could also be a symbol of Christ, who was often depicted in medieval religious stories as a hart and is described in the Bible as " the Lion of Judah". The cover depicted here dated from 1790, and was installed by Dr. Leman, then the rector, who also paid for a new pulpit and flooring. There used to be a fresco of St. Christopher over the north door of the church, which must have dated from pre-Reformation times. It was believed that whoever beheld the image of St. Christopher, "on that day shall not faint or fall," thanks to the prayers of the saint. It was rediscovered in 1906 during repairs, and had evidently remained on view until the 1800s, as an old woman who died in 1905 remembered seeing it as a child – although she remembered it as a giant, bearing a flowering staff in his hand, with a large fish at his feet.

Mill Common (depicted here) straddled London Road in a diamond shape and was named after the mill which had stood to the right. There were several large commons in Pakefield such as Runnel Heath, where the industrial estate is sited, which were enclosed in 1799 and divided up between the local landowners. The enclosure of commons enabled them to be cultivated, but removed a means of sustenance for the poor, who previously were able to graze their animals there. A smaller plot was set aside for Trustees to provide for the poor.In the background is Wellington Road, which was developed in or soon after 1897 by George Elsey of Kirkley. At this time the field was purchased by the Lowestoft Steam Herring Drifters Company Ltd of Waveney Chambers, who used it to dry nets on.

There were nine major farms in Pakefield, some many hundreds of years old. The White House, Stradbroke Road was part of a 134 acre estate in Kirkley which in the early 1800s was owned by Rev. John Grieve Spurgeon, passing to his daughter Frances Elizabeth Acton (who gave her name to Acton Road) in 1830. Frances Acton, let the farm and estate (in Kirkley) out to John Matchet, a Pakefield farmer, who owned all the land between the church and Arbour Lane, and lived in a farm house located in Florence Road. The white house became a hotel, which in 1924, was owned by Mrs. H Grimble, and in 1936, was run by Mrs. G Lang.

The Kirkley side of Pakefield Street, the parish boundary ran down the centre of the road. Very early in the history of Pakefield and Kirkley, the population became concentrated along here, probably because most people were involved in fishing. In 1841 there was a smattering of trades such as a baker, a shoe maker, carpenters and bricklayers. However, most people were fishermen. There were also coopers, sailmakers and shipwrights whose livelihoods also depended on the sea. Fisher folk had a professional approach to their work, despite their poverty: an observer writing in the 22nd January 1862 *Norwich Mercury* noted that while their homes in Pakefield Street were not especially clean or comfortable, "all things relating to the sea occupation were certainly square and taut." In 1841 there were 495 residents of Pakefield and 416 of Kirkley. Pakefield Street turned left at the end of this row of houses into Pakefield Road, the route taken by the London to Yarmouth mail coach until the 1790s. Beyond the last house were the tall cliffs and the sea. In 1812 the view from the cliffs was described as "strikingly grand and beautiful. Here, the globe we inhabit seems divided, and eastward and westward equal parts of water and land are beheld." A different perspective was offered by the new curate Rev. Hoare on his arrival in Pakefield in 1836, describing it as "a bleak village on the top of a cliff."

These cottages were mostly let out. The furthest away building was the Mill Inn. Until 1833 auctions were held there and it was where the Pakefield Beach Company had their meetings. It is thought to be named after a mill that had been nearby until it fell into the sea. A number of the nearer houses were owned by Abraham Scales, who also owned a shop that stood on the other side of the street. From the 1600s until 1845 the shop was run by the Scales family and sold tea, grocery, china, glass, linen and woollens as well as being the chemists. He sold it in 1845 to Mr Robert Johnson. Sadly for him it didn't prove a success, for in 1847 a newspaper reported that Robert Johnson was bankrupted and his stock and house were to be sold.

On the other side of Pakefield Street, at the very end was the old Manor House, which overlooked a few cottages and sheds on the cliff edge and faced out to sea. The site was for many years occupied by several families – in 1841 the families of John Adams, Mary Wright and John Fisher were tenants. The site was owned by the Lord of Bacon's Manor at Gorleston. The house in the photograph was built in the 1890s by combining two existing houses for Mr. Hudson a coal merchant from Norfolk.

Looking towards Pakefield Road with the Manor House on the right. In 1871 plans were approved for several houses and a hotel to be built at the south west corner of Pakefield Road. These houses, behind the Cliff Hotel were Rochester Terrace, built in 1872, a row of seven terraced houses plus Ingle Nook, which now overlooks the car park. The Cliff Hotel was one of the earlier hotel developments in Pakefield, and was owned by Bullards, the Norwich brewer founded in 1837.

Thomas Hastings was the publican from 1886 until 1900, when John W Atkins took over. John Atkins is the one leaning on the door in 1906, when he was 42. He was born in Cosford, Leicestershire, was married to Jane Elliot from Lowestoft and had six sons. His career had taken him to Flixton before he took over the Jolly Sailors.

11

Looking inland from the end of Pakefield Street. The gardens on the right remain today, as does the cottage, but the nearest houses on the left are on the site of what is now a car park overlooking the sea. The house with the bay windows was from around 1861 Pakefield Post Office and was known as Bow House. In the early 1800s, it was the old Rectory occupied by Rev. Francis Cunningham. It was a large house, owned by Abraham Scales, with four sitting rooms, seven bedrooms, attics, cellars and offices and had a walled garden, barn and stable. Beyond Bow House ran the lane that became known as Beach Street. Beyond that was a house occupied by Rev. Cunningham's curate. A friend of William Wilerforce Rev. Cunningham was rector at Pakefield from 1814 to 1856, and at St. Margaret's, Lowestoft from 1831 to 1863. He and his wife Richenda had a profound impact on the fisherfolk of Pakefield, through their affection and care for their flock, as well as powerful Bible reading.

Describing the services that Rev. and Mrs. Cunningham held at the church, her nephew Edward Hoare wrote, ' Mr. Cunningham's church services, I have heard, were very comfortable and homely. On Sunday evenings especially, when the lamps burnt bright and warm in the church, and the parishioners came trooping into their seats, and the sea-wind moaned without – then was the time for Aunt Cunningham to enjoy herself among her flock. Evening church was infinitely grateful and satisfying to them all – a cheerful, sociable scene, with the bright lamp-light falling on all the well-known faces, rosy in the pleasant warmth after a cold walk. They rise from their knees, Aunt Cunningham and her friends, and settle themselves in their places with beaming looks, disposing their preparations about them, their wraps and Bibles and hymn-books, for an hour that is the treat of the whole week. "Here we all are again," they seem to say, radiantly glancing. "Now!" – and off they go in a fine florid hymn-tune, "Helmsley" hope, with plenty of trailing sweeps up to high notes, in which enjoyment can really give tongue.

Cunningham rented the white house in the centre of the picture for his nephew and curate, Edward Hoare. Further down the street is the house where Cunningham founded a school for Pakefield children, which eventually spread to three sites in Pakefield Street. On the left, where the horse and cart have drawn up was the butchers shop of J Wright. It was the eighth building listed from the cliff in Pakefield Street in 1871, when all of the houses closer to the cliff were occupied by fishing families (Thompson, Adams, Allen, and Mullender).

The entrance to Beach Street, where in 1861 there was a shoe making industry. James Mickleburgh, a master shoemaker, employed eight men and two boys, and lived in a house on the right. 72 Pakefield Street, the bow window shop in the left foreground was a grocers, occupied by Charles Rush, which in April 1908 was burnt down. At about 1.30 am, Mr. Allen, a neighbour, saw flames and went for the fire brigade and police. The fire brigade steamer fought the blaze until 5 am. The stock, worth £300, was completely destroyed. In 1905 a Pakefield Street inhabitant recalled that in his childhood, "There was a pub, the original Jolly Sailors [on the left beyond the tree]. Further along was a fish curing business of Mr. George Hazell, where you could buy the best bloaters at two for one and a half pennies. Mr. Rush kept a grocers shop. Mrs. Jessie Lincoln kept a small sweet shop. Mr. Fred Craik was the butcher. Mr. Billy Bullen was the baker. Then there was the Old Ship Inn. Mr. Rouse was the greengrocer. Mrs. Wright had the pork butcher shop; she had an old grandfather clock which kept perfect time, kids used to look in there any time they wanted to know the time. Mr. West was the cobbler." Nearly all of these buildings have since gone.

All the buildings to the right from the bend have since been demolished. One of these was the bakers shop owned by William George Davy, who in 1869 was accused, with his wife Susannah, of trying to poison his brother with arsenic. The brothers had been partners in a bakery business in Pakefield, but John moved to Swaffham and became a miller. Their mother died and left her property in equal portions to her sons. John went to London to receive his own and his brother's share of the legacy. On his way back he spent a few days with his brother at Pakefield. Before he left Mrs. Davy gave him six small currant cakes. John ate three of

them when he got home and felt no ill effects, but while eating a fourth cake he remarked to his landlady, Mrs. Harvey, that the cake contained some white specks in it. He was taken very ill. The doctor was called and said John was suffering from the effects of poisoning. The remainder of the cake was analysed and found to contain a great quantity of arsenic. In court the theory of the prosecution was that William and his wife wished to take possession of the second share of the mother's legacy. The cake was analysed at Guy's Hospital and mercury was found to be in it which could be found in ointment for ringworm, and in powder to destroy vermin in dogs. The defence submitted that the powder had been mistaken for baking powder. In summing up the judge pointed out to the jury that supposing they thought that one of the two prisoners intentionally put the poison in the cake, it would be very difficult to say which one of them it was, for though the wife made the cakes, the husband might have put the poison in after the dough had been apportioned. The jury acquitted the prisoners. The Davys remained in Pakefield until at least 1871 as bakers, so presumably the local population felt it was safe enough to eat their wares.

The trees on the right are in the grounds of the Society of Friends. There had been Quakers in Pakefield and Kirkley for hundreds of years, with the Scales family being leading members, who supported the work in very practical ways. Mary Scales in 1826 for example owned a property in Kirkley that she said in her will the Friends could use for just 1 shilling per year. The relationship between the rector and the Quakers had not always been so cordial. In 1731 John Scales was prosecuted by Rev. Philip Richardson for failing to pay his tithes, and only avoided prison after another rector offered to pay the outstanding sum.

Pakefield Street, which was called High Street on the 1861 census, had fishermen, shops, seven shoemakers and two laundresses. On the right are two old houses – the nearest was occupied in 1841 by Thomas Redgrave (aged 50, agricultural labourer), with his wife Martha and daughter Esther (aged 19). The next was split into two apartments, one occupied by Samuel Martin (fisherman), his wife Mary (aged 24) and baby Henry Lincoln Martin; the other occupied by Amos Lincoln (44 year old bricklayer) and his wife Rachel Lincoln (aged 45). By 1861 this had become the Trowel and Hammer pub, run by Rachel. It is advertising Lacons' Yarmouth Stout and Dinner Ale. Lacons began brewing in 1760 in Yarmouth, and by 1920 had 350 tied houses in East Anglia and London. May Terrace, the row of houses on the left opposite the Trowel and Hammer, was built in 1893.

Near the Trowel and Hammer pub was Church Road, now known as All Saints Road. On the corner of St. Georges Road was a dairy, just beyond where car LA 3908 is driving, and there used to be a laundry beyond that. In 1841, this was all agricultural land, part of Blacksmith Field. The wooden building on the right was a fisherman's shed, or chandlers and just a few of the houses on the left were built before 1880. Nearly everything else was built in the 1880s.

The blacksmiths shop in the 1840s belonged to William Everett, a farmer who owned an estate running right from Pakefield Street up to Claremont Road. He lived in Morris' Farm in Carlton Road near Kirkley Church. The blacksmith then was William Allen. Next to the smithy is Pump Alley, which is an old lane that ran along the edge of Blacksmith Field up to Walmer Cottage, to give it access to Pakefield Street. In 1851 Henry Moyce became blacksmith and after him Joseph Hephur took over as wheelright. He is shown here tending to a broken cart.

On the right, hidden behind the trees, is the house where Elizabeth and John Rolph lived. His wonderful second hand bookshop in the old coach house is a memory that will stay with many for life. That had been the Manor House, Kirkley. An ancient mulberry tree in the back garden was possibly planted in the 17th century when the production of silk was being encouraged.

Roughly opposite the blacksmiths, at the top of the Causeway, was one of the Cunningham Schools built at Rev. Cunningham's own expense. In 1861 it listed as the Boys School, by 1871 it had to be replaced because it was in a dilapidated state and was severely overcrowded. The new schoolopened in 1871 with just under 100 children attending the first day. At first there were a lot of visitors and the children had to stop work and rise up to greet them. This caused chaos, and after three months of slates getting broken, ink being spilled and copybooks blotted, this politeness was disposed of. Over the years the school increased to such an extent that it too was very overcrowded. Three children sat together on seats made for two and the rows were five deep. Several inspectors complained about the overcrowding and unhealthy, hot environment, as well as noting that, "the first class scholars seem unintelligent, and not to know the meaning of two words they use. "They concluded that "Pakefield appears to swarm with children." Illness spread rapidly around the crowded school and both children and adults sucumbed to such diseases as smallpox, croop, scarlatina, scarlet fever, mumps, whooping cough, diphtheria and typhoid fever. Deaths due to these were common, and can't have been helped by the Pakefield School Cesspools, which even in 1904 still stank in the school grounds. Eventually this very crowded overpopulated school was closed and Pakefield Primary School took over.

There was an annual school treat for the children to encourage them to attend more regularly, as the children were perpetually taken out of school for long periods to work – in July 1871 several children were away because they were haymaking and thinning beet and in January 1872 children returned after 7 months absence to attend the fishing, the boys for the sea and wharf work and the girls for mending the nets. The children basically attended when it suited them, and when Pinders Circus was expected, or Buffalo Bill's Wild West Show came then the children were off school like a shot. Likewise when there were cliff falls in 1891 many school boys went searching for fossils and coins among the fall of debris. Things didn't change and in September 1901 it was recorded that "children continue to attend school just when they please, without action taken to enforce regular attendance. Some children are still away visiting friends and others are attending to the wants of visitors." One treat was in the fields at the back of Stradbrook Road. Hundreds attended, the little ones travelling in wagons. In 1871 230 children left the school at 2.45pm, had tea in the fields and played until 8.15 when the children walked in procession back to the village. Other locations for the treat were Normanston, the Rectory Garden, and the farm of Sidney Smith (where 415 had tea and played games in the 1880s).

For centuries Pakefield and Kirkley focused on the sea, the wide beach being ideal for drawing up fishing boats. The inhabitants were engaged in fishing and from the 17th century, salvage work – which developed into running the lifeboat (the large vessel in the picture). The bulk of the population of both parishes lived along Pakefield Street. From the Street the inhabitants could get easy access to the beach, along a rugged, sandy pathway which threaded down the steep cliff, and to their fleet of boats, yawls and other craft. The sheds on the cliff stand on what became known as "Boathouse Piece", land which had been given to Emmanuel College, Cambridge in 1674 by Ann Hunt, in order to fund the education of two poor students from Suffolk. By the 1820s the land was eroding and becoming unfit for agricultural purposes, so in 1831 it was rented to the Beach Company, at the request of Rev. Cunningham.

Unloading a catch of sprats from LT 45. The rhythm of the fishing meant that different fish were available throughout the year. Sprats were caught from December to January, soon after the herring season (September to November) concluded. Mackerel were caught in May and June. At other times of the year, some of the more enterprising fished for deep water fish. During the 16th century, the Dutch became pre-eminent in North Sea fishing, and were so successful that many English fishermen simply went to sea to purchase their catch from the Dutch, to sell it back ashore! In 1524 there were three Dutchmen living in Pakefield and Kirkley (Garrard Garradson, Orte Johnson and Josse Couper), as well as three Scots, two Bretons and a Frenchman. The pattern was similar in Lowestoft and Kessingland. The success of the Dutch was a cause of great complaint and envy to many in England, who feared that England's naval prowess would diminish if the fishing did not flourish, but a study of the wills of Pakefield and Kirkley people throughout the 1600s shows that plenty of people were still engaging in fishing, not just locally, but also in the longer distance fishing up towards Iceland – and many men and women had shares in boats, or supplied the nets, meaning they could enjoy a share of the catch. In the years before the 1840s, the larger boats tended to be kept on Lowestoft Beach or even at Yarmouth. Many of the wealthier inhabitants of Pakefield and Kirkley had business interests in these places, such as Nathaniel Colby, of Pakefield, who was master of the *Martin*, a 43 ton boat with crew of twelve and engaged in herring fishing.

Mrs. Tommy Turrell, Mrs. Ethel Smith and Mrs. Dick Barker of Kessingland are making the nets ready to use. On both sides of the North Sea, and all along the coast, women played an important role in mending or "beating" the nets, as well as gutting and packing herring. Many women also owned shares in boats.

Fishing nets are laid out on the sand to dry alongside the little fishing boats. Fishermen have drawn their boats up onto the beach in this way for many hundreds of years. Nets were taken great care of, since their owners were entitled to a share of the catch, even though they might not have a share in the fishing boat, or be able to go to sea. Many women owned nets in the 17th century, and thereby had some means of living. Herring nets were frequently damaged by dogfish that got caught in them while eating herring.

It has been said that Mr. and Mrs. James Thompson lived on Pakefield Beach in a house made from a boat cut in half with the ends pointing upwards. This is a reminder of the harshness of life for those who could not afford even to rent a cottage in the village. Some Pakefield men were rough and coarse – men like John Manclarke of Pakefield who in 1733 was a pilot employed by Trinity House, to guide ships through difficult seaways along the coast. Unfortunately he was given to drink, had little respect for the rules, and was frequently summoned to court for bad behaviour. On one occasion, while piloting His Majesty's ship *Fly*, he fell out with the Lieutenant and gunner of that ship, saying he, "Did not care a fart for them" and going away he told them to tell the captain that, "He might kiss his arse", and a great deal more. He was eventually stripped of his pilot's licence, due to incidents such as these.

Old yawl, upturned and used as a shed for beachmen. Depicted are Dixon Peek and Cluff Fisher. The Napoleonic Wars may have prompted local fishermen to organise themselves into beach companies. Because fishing was an important occupation, they were exempt from impressment into the Navy, but in 1798 the Admiralty formed the Sea Fencibles, who were trained under the command of naval officers, to protect the coast from French invasion. They served as coastguards, performed coastal patrol and manned coastal signal stations and small boats. Several Pakefield men trained at Benacre under the command of Martin Hinton Esq. Captain. They were taught to fire guns and work as a team (although not always successfully; in May 1798 Robert Fuller and Henry Fisher of Pakefield were both killed when the gun they were loading went off unexpectedly). They were able to put this training into practice when, in 1807 they saved 121 soldiers of the 28th Regiment when the *Peace* in which they were travelling got into difficulty. For this act they were commended by the Admiralty and paid 121 Guineas. It was in 1807 or thereabouts that William Colby formed the Pakefield Beach Company, whose eighteen or so members were known as the "roaring boys" (an allusion to their fishing occupation: the word stems from the Dutch term "roeren", referring to "stirring" herrings in salt to preserve them). Between them they owned a yawl, *Friends' Adventure*, which had a crew of twelve, and in 1809 its master was Thomas Colby.

A scene from 1833, before Lowestoft Harbour was constructed, with Kirkley cliffs in the background, showing a large vessel being built or repaired on the beach. The sea was a source of income from fishing, but also for other, illicit, means of getting wealthy. Throughout much of the 18th century, high taxes on imported luxuries made smuggling a profitable business, and at least some of the local population engaged in this. As early as 1704 the revenue collector at Yarmouth recommended that an additional officer be stationed at Pakefield because of the amount of smuggling going on. It was big business. Indeed, in 1733 it was reported that "considerable numbers of armed men appear weekly on this coast near to Lowestoft and Pakefield and carry off great quantities of tea and prohibited goods, and appear in so formidable manner" that the government officers dared not attack them! One of the ships known to be landing contraband at Benacre was *Colby's cutter* – which suggests it was owned by a Pakefield man, Colby being a local name. On 4th Feb 1734 it was stated in Parliament, "All the young, clever Suffolk fellows were employed by smugglers and have 2 shillings and 6 pence a day while waiting, and a guinea a day when disposing of goods by horseback about country. Gangs 40-50 strong." There was also a pub at Kirkley kept by James Saunders, a huge old boy of the very rough and ready type, who was known as the king of smugglers, and whose house was, in his latter days, the rendezvous of all who liked to hear him tell tales of adventures at sea, or along shore, of those who lived by bluffing or outwitting the Preventive officers. The Pakefield men were not all involved in smuggling all the time, however, and in 1819, while trawling for anchors, a crew accidentally brought up 112 casks of brandy and gin, which they hurriedly took to the custom officers at Yarmouth. This must have been a sad blow to someone, though!

Throughout most of its life, the Pakefield Beach Company made use of yawls, clinker built, flexible and with shallow draught able to work in most winds and weathers. It seems to have derived from an ancient boatbuilding tradition, going back to the longboats of the Vikings, but was a design that was perfected in the 19th century. The names given to their boats tend to reflect the nature of the beachmen's work – *Rescue*, *Welcome Home*, *Happy Return* – are female names – *Janette*, *Clara* or in the case of the yawl built in 1890 for the re-formed Company – *Sir Savile Crossley* – probably reflecting the name of who paid for the boat. In their yawls, the Roaring Boys carried on brisk business, regularly going out to help vessels in difficulty and vigorously fending off their competitors. They were experienced, tough and very successful, growing by 1882 to a company of 70 men. The rules of the beach companies governed how the earnings were to be distributed. Generally each member had a share in the company, which he could mortgage, sell or bequeath to his widow or other relative in the event of death. However, only those who were of suitable quality were allowed to go out to sea – and had to be approved by the Coxswain, who was in charge of the men while at sea. The rules of salvage meant that an abandoned ship – where neither man nor animal remained on board – was worth more than one still with crew. The first salvors to get to a vessel in difficulty and board it (and remain on board) had the claim to the salvage, so there was often fierce competition between villages, with several companies racing to be the first to get to a wreck to claim it. When several companies arrived at once, there could be violence to decide who would remain in possession of the prize, and in any event whatever the captain of a ship in trouble may have agreed to in the heat of the moment, there was a good chance he would dispute it when safely on shore. Finally, therefore, there could be litigation in the courts, since any claim for salvage had to be made in the Admiralty Court. In order to be best represented, the companies usually had an agent, but much of the advocacy was done by the beachmen themselves.

Beach Street in 1926. This lane ran from beside the Rectory in Pakefield Street down to Boathouse Piece, formerly known as Barn Close. It was here in 1840 that the lifeboat station was established by the RNLI, although it was run by the locals. The houses depicted were occupied in the 1840s by some of the prominent Beachmen, such as Nathaniel Colby, (whose cottage later became the tea shop we see here), Robert Lincoln, William Warford, Edward Peek and George Lewis.

At the end of Beach Street, on the cliff edge, just next to Boathouse Piece, William Everett built a pub that was run in the 1840s by Edmund English. It was known as the Good Woman, then the Morning Star, and finally the Oddfellows Arms. For a time during the 1860s, the landlord was George Meek Warford, the Cox'n of the Pakefield Lifeboat, who lived there with his wife Griselda and eight children. This pub can be seen on the left of the picture. During the 1860s, the two fields next to this pub, between Beach Street and the cliff were developed as housing. The street facing out to sea that is depicted here was known as Cliff Cottages. It was inhabited in 1871 mainly by Colbys – fishermen and fish merchants. The light coloured building in the centre was the Lord Nelson Pub, run in 1871 by Emmanuel Colby. The house marked "where I was born" was known as "Sea View Cottage", occupied by 78 year old William Colby and his second wife Sarah (aged 68).

The baker's shop on the right was in 1871 run by George Chandler. Opposite, on the left by the lamp post, is what is now the Jolly Sailors Pub. It was for many years a fisherman's cottage and garden. In 1871 it was being run as a pub by John Bird, who was also a joiner, and in 1891, the publican was John Atkins, who in 1898 went to take over the Cliff Hotel, which can be seen right at the end of the Street. When this was built, the licence of the old Mill Inn (which had some time before been washed away) was transferred to this site. The beachmen used to meet in the Mill Inn, but on its demise, they moved to the old Ship Inn, seen on the right of the picture. The interior of the Ship Inn in 1862 was described as having a "cabin-look," smelling of pitch and tar, and had a collection of block pullies for small vessels in a corner, a broken oar in another, and a compass case without a needle hanging from a shelf. Here also hung a copy of the Company's twelve rules, designed in a Biblical style (headed *"Village of Joppa, 2m., 8 day, 30th Year Christ aevi. Rules. Zebedee, Father of Fishermen"* – a reference to the father of James and John, fishermen disciples of Jesus).

The rules, which give us a precious insight into the professional and moral life of the beachmen, ran as follows.

1. Those only who attend the sett to share with those who launch the ship [this appears to refer to laying nets, and may therefore be an old rule to do with dividing the earnings from fishing].
2. Fifteen Elders to deliberate on all matters of importance – their decision to be final.
3. No swearing or gossiping.
4. Six days shalt thou labour. Keep holy the seventh day. Honour they father and mother.
5. Whatever thy earnings shalt be, thou shalt give to the Aged and Infirm a share.
6. A vacancy in the company by ballot.
7. No two Elders to speak at the same time.
8. The young and inexperienced to place confidence in the Elders, who are bound to be just.
9. Four Elders to form a Board – not less.
10. In case any person shall be employed on company's business [presumably such matters as attending court to enter claims for salvage, or otherwise dealing with commercial transactions], to be allowed a share of anything during his or her absence.
11. Eleventh Commandment – *sine qua non*.
12. In saving life, the money to be earned to be divided, half to those who float, and half to those who attend the shore.

(signed) *Zebedee*.

According to the landlady of the Ship Inn in 1862, the rules were written down "a long time off now" by the then keeper of the Pakefield lighthouse, possibly George Goodwin. The type of rescue referred to in Rule 12 was illustrated by a painting "to commemorate the winter of 1834," which was remembered as "a sad one, for there was no end to wrecks and calamities of all kinds here." The painting showed the high sandy cliff of Pakefield, with the rough sea below, and in the distance a sinking vessel. Several figures were depicted struggling in the waves, one of them being rescued by a man in seaman's garb (one of the Roaring Boys), with a line fastened round his waist, which was held by a comrade on the cliff summit.

The rescuer in the painting, Henry Colby, saved many lives, but died in Hull, where he had been taken out of the cabin of a vessel "stark staring mad." Above the whole of the fireplace, was a further painting, but this one of a tomb shaped as a stunted pyramid, with Lowestoft Church in the background, inscribed "to the memory of Robert Peek and his crew, drowned 30th October 1836." Peek was a Pakefield man and the captain of a vessel. However, he, his son and most of his crew were drowned before they could even get out of their berths – a reminder of the cruelty of the sea.

One route used to get into Lowestoft Harbour was the Pakefield Gat, a channel of two fathoms depth at low tide, which from 1831 was marked by buoys and a red light on the cliff. It was a dangerous channel, which shifted and caused many a wreck. The board of Trinity House soon decided to erect a permanent lighthouse at Pakefield and in August 1831 agreed that James Taylor of Yarmouth should build it. The lighthouse was positioned a bit inland, due to coastal erosion taking place. A road was built to reach it and in doing that work Mr. Robert Lee's horse fell over the cliff. In October 1831 George Medmer Goodwin was appointed keeper of the light, being paid £65 as "salary, gratuity and allowance for beer", and the light first shone on 15th May 1832. By 1833 the Stanford channel had become highly dangerous to shipping due to sand building up. Mr. Davies in his report to the board of Trinity House suggested, "That this worthless crooked channel ought to be abandoned and all the buoys in it. "On 3rd December 1864, Trinity House published a warning to mariners that due to the occurrence of several wrecks in the Pakefield Gat, that way had become unsafe at night, and so the red light on the cliff would not be exhibited until further notice. Ships' masters were cautioned that the Gat was not safe for vessels drawing more than fourteen feet of water. By 1886, the Gat had moved, such that there was a need for a new position for the red light – which was sited in a shed on the cliff in the Cliftonville Estate.  This was soon replaced by a red light in the Pakefield Lighthouse again, which remained in use until 1907, when its function was replaced by gas buoys (which could more conveniently be relocated with the shifting of the sea floor). On its discontinuance in 1907, it was auctioned off with the keeper's cottage and sold for £120, for conversion into a seaside bungalow. It was still there in July 1910, when it was moved back 100 yards owing to the erosion of the coast at that point. The framing and outside covering were described as being of iron, whilst inside there were brick divisional walls and plaster ceilings. The complete building which weighed 60 – 70 tons, was moved bodily upon a cradle constructed for moving Lowestoft Low light, the haulage being effected by a crab.

Pakefield Lifeboat House, before Claremont Pier was built in 1903, with the Grand Hotel on the left. The lifeboats are perhaps the epitome of selfless devotion to the rescue of lives, but the origins of this institution, certainly on the east coast, are tied up with the work of the beachmen.

In 1892, James Banes Swan commented to the *Lowestoft Journal* that "when I was a little boy 70 years ago [1822] the Pakefield men were the chaps to save life. Take 'em all round they were the finest race of men along the coast."

Sometimes the sea was just too rough to launch a rescue boat. For this reason, Captain Manby invented his "lifesaving apparatus," a kind of mortar that launched a rocket trailing a rope. The rocket was aimed to fly over the stricken ship and the endangered crew could cling to the rope, which was fastened on the shore and haul themselves to safety.

As the 19th century progressed, many felt that the business of saving lives should be put on a more organised footing – both by providing lifeboats which could better withstand rough seas, and by rewarding the beachmen specifically for saving lives, not just for saving property. The first purpose built lifeboat was stationed at Lowestoft in 1801, at the impetus of Robert Sparrow. However, this boat was considered to be unsuitable for work off the coast of Suffolk, as it took too long to launch. It was not until 1807, with the building, of the specially-designed *Frances Ann* by Lionel Lukin, that the locals were willing to use the lifeboat. This was a wholly new design based on the local yawls, but fitted with empty casks in order to make it unsubmersible, and was the origin of the "Norfolk and Suffolk" type of lifeboat. It was placed under the control of the Suffolk Humane Society, formed in Kessingland in 1806. There was no lifeboat crew except the beachmen who were paid to man it. For many years the Suffolk Humane Society was so poor that it was a struggle to reward the beachmen properly for their efforts – so that on a number of occasions the £5 paid by the Society was augmented by the generosity of local worthies. The RNLI, who took over, paid 10s for a day launch and £1 by night, on the strict understanding that the lifeboat was not to be used to salvage property, but only to save lives – and should only be launched when life was already in danger. In consequence, where there was a good prospect of reward from salvage, the beachmen preferred to launch their own company yawl – which led on 12th November 1852 to there being no crew for the Lowestoft lifeboat, because the men had already gone off in Lowestoft Company yawls to assist another wreck. The conflict between saving life and financial reward led to tension between beachmen and lifeboat – such as on 7th December 1821, when the brig *Westmoreland* was wrecked on the Newcome Sand. A number of yawls, as well as the Lowestoft Lifeboat set off to the rescue, and the *Seaman's Assistance* got there first. When the lifeboat under Lieutenant Harmer arrived, and the crew of the *Westmoreland* tried to get on board, John Stebbings from the *Seaman's Assistance* cut the line, saying "They'd no business here! The ship is ours – we've got the job. We're your safeguards and protectors – why you're as safe as if you were ashore – and we'll take you ashore." However, for some reason they only took two passengers ashore. In the darkness it then became impossible to make contact with the brig, and when Lieutenant Harmer, clearly very concerned, launched a skiff from Pakefield Beach at 1 am, he found only two men still alive. Having climbed into the rigging to help them, he also met with disaster when his skiff was washed away. Fortunately a Pakefield boat arrived, and Lieutenant Harmer was able to help the two men into it, before climbing in himself.

With so many wrecks along the coast, a lifeboat, was needed at Pakefield too. In 1841 Pakefield's first lifeboat, *Marianne*, was built in Northumberland. She had fourteen oars, and was 46 feet 3 inches long by 12 feet wide and was coxed by Nathaniel Colby. The cost, together with a shed to keep her in, around £400, was financed through local subscriptions. On many occasions the Pakefield and Lowestoft Lifeboats worked together to save lives. Eventually the beach companies transformed into the lifeboat crew, and the lifeboat became the main means by which the beachmen made their living.

The Sisters was built in 1872 by Samuel Sparham of Lowestoft at a cost of £276. She wa was 46 feet and 3 inches and had twelve oars and was the gift of the Misses Sarah and Lydia Harris and the late Mr. T Perkins of Wighton, Norfolk. In 1876 she was renamed as *The Two Sisters Mary and Hannah* and served at the Pakefield No. 1 lifeboat station from 1872 to 1886, before moving to Lowestoft No. 2 station from 1886 to 1890. In 1890 she returned to Pakefield No. 1 station until 1910, when she was sold by the RNLI. She saved a total of 163 people; 145 while on the Pakefield station. Nathaniel Colby continued from the *Marianne* to be the coxswain of the new lifeboat from 1872 to 1876, when George Warford took over, who was coxwain until 1898. He was the grandson of John Warford, landlord of the Ship Inn. He died in 1923 aged 89 years and his coffin was carried by the coxwains of the lifeboats at Pakefield, Southwold, Lowestoft, Caister, Kessingland, Gorleston, Cromer and Aldborough. His gravestone in Pakefield Churchyard bears the inscription, "Safe home in port." During his lifeboat service of 33 years he helped to save 396 lives, not just in his lifeboat, but also with other yawls and craft.

Samuel Martin followed George as coxswain from 1899 to 1910. John Ward was elected undercoxwain, Albert Chapman bowman and J W Colby as signalman. It was hard to keep the lifeboat going, so the crew organised regular fund-raising events. At one in 1908, when the crew demonstrated launching the boat down this score, a nasty accident occurred, as it swerved and crushed one of the onlookers, Mr. Edward Chapman of 22 Rochester Road, Kirkley against the bank. He was given first aid by the Boys Brigade, then taken to hospital by wagon with a crushed leg. The lifeboat itself carried on down the slope, and went off under full sail to Lowestoft Harbour. There the crew formed a procession behind the Boys Brigade band, collecting money, before returning to Pakefield.

When Sam Martin became coxswain, the lifeboat still belonged to the Pakefield Beach Company. In 1910 the company had a new 42 foot long boat. Samuel Martin did not live to see the launch as on the day it was scheduled to occur was the day of his funeral. The picture shows the funeral procession leaving his house (40, St. Georges Road). The coffin was covered with the Pakefield Beach Company's flag, bore his lifebelt and a number of wreaths. The hearse was preceded by the Pakefield lifeboat crew and several members of the Beach Company and was followed by members of the deceased's family, including his brothers and sisters and his four children. Following the service in the church the remains were conveyed to the graveside by six members of the crew of the Pakefield Lifeboat.

Courtesy Port of Lowestoft Research Society collection.

The *James Leath* was at Pakefield from 1910 to 1919 and was the legacy of James Leath of Winchmore Hill London. She was a wooden Norfolk and Suffolk type pulling and sailing lifeboat, built by Thames Ironworks, Blackwall, London in 1910. After she left Pakefield in 1919 she went to Caister No. 1 station until 1928, then to Aldeburgh No. 2 until 1935. The RNLI sold her in 1935 and she was converted to a yacht. While at Pakefield a total of 20 people were saved.

Courtesy of Port of Lowestoft Research Society collection.

Hugh Taylor was also a wooden Norfolk and Suffolk type pulling and sailing lifeboat and was the gift of Mrs. Elizabeth Streatfield of Mayfair, London. She was built in 1912 by Thames Ironworks, Blackwall, London at a cost of £1250. Here she is depicted on regatta day. Before serving Pakefield she was at Great Yarmouth No.2 station from 1912 until 1919. JL Ward was the lifeboat coxswain until 1922, when the lifeboat was moved to Lowestoft to become part of the Reserve fleet. In 1929 she went to Aldeburgh No. 2 station for two years, when she moved on to Kessingland No 1 station. She was only launched three times at Pakefield. She was sold by the RNLI in 1936 and converted into a yacht.

Even while the beachmen and the lifeboat were rescuing sailors, their way of life was passing. The beginning of the end for the beach companies was the establishment of tugs stationed in the harbour. These tended to carry out the easier salvage operations, while the beachmen manning the lifeboat were called to the most dangerous rescues. This caused tremendous friction. In 1850 the Lowestoft beachmen came to blows with the crew of the tug *Lowestoft* for undercutting them in their rescue work, and in 1859 the Pakefield beachmen took legal action when the tug *Powerful* stole the job of pulling the *Lisbon* off the Newcome Sands. This came just three years after a litigated case where the Pakefield beachmen went out to rescue the sloop *Elizabeth*. At 5am the sloop was in difficulty, and hoisted a flag for a steam tug. However, the tug did not come, so the beachmen launched their yawl with 24 crew, and for a fee of £200 got the sloop to safe anchorage. At 5pm the tug finally left the hatbour and towed the *Elizabeth* to harbour, whereupon the captain of that vessel disputed the beachmen's entitlement to the £200. When the case got to court the beachmen only got £65, and had to pay their own costs. The harbour, the railways, and steam boats meant there were far fewer wrecks which meant so much less income for the beachmen. The numbers of rescues, decreased over time. 1922, with the closure of the lifeboat station, marked the end of a way of life in Pakefield. However, the harbour provided the opportunity to use larger fishing boats, and so fishing became more profitable. Many Pakefield and Kirkley men worked from Lowestoft Harbour on smacks.

LT 299 *Olive* and LT 416. *Olive* was built in 1901 by H Reynolds of Lowestoft, but for many years of her life, was owned by Pakefield men – James Adams of Pakefield Street was master and owner of *Olive* from 1903 to 1906, then Thomas Cole of Payne Street, Kirkley owned her from 1906 to 1907, and J Cole of Florence Road Pakefield owned her from 1911 to 1912. She was eventually sold to Sweden in 1931.

The fishing fleet returning to harbour. There was great competition to get back first with the catch, to get the best prices. There were many Scottish fishermen in the fleet, who had strong religious views on not fishing on a Sunday. It was their practice to come back together Saturday morning in time for the auction, attend church – such as the Bethel – and just after midnight early Monday morning, to sail out together again. The smack was developed by Thames boat builders in Barking, Gravesend and Greenwich in the early 1800s. By 1852 Barking alone had 134 sailing trawlers as well as 46 smacks. On the east coast, Lowestoft was a great rival to Yarmouth: in 1852 it gained independence as a fishing port in its own right and over the next decades built up a fishing fleet that was bigger than Yarmouth's – having 300 to 400 sailing trawlers by 1900.

Increased competition encouraged fishermen to stay out at sea longer and sail further into the North Sea to find richer fishing grounds. By sorting their fish on board, fish could be packed in ice and transferred onto steamers. and fishing fleets could stay out at sea for many weeks at a time. Little rowing boats transported boxes of fish from the smack to a steam vessel which quickly took them to Lowestoft. This dangerous activity cost many fishermen their lives. Frequently accidents occurred, particularly in rough weather, when boats jostled each other to get alongside, climbing on and off the steamer, or handing boxes up.

In the 1870s and 1880s. East coast fishermen were plagued by attacks on their fishing nets by Belgian and Dutch fishing vessels. Not only would they rip and damage their nets with large metal hooks, named Devils, but they had the audacity to offer to sell them back to the English fishermen!! Parliament had an inquiry, led by W H Higgins QC, on the outrages of foreigners on English fishermen in the North Sea, and culprits were taken to court. Mostly attacks took place at night.

Four Royal Navy steam cruisers, HMS *Ariel*, *Redwing*, *Firefly* and *Hearty* and one schooner, the *Mermaid*, and two cutters, the *Beaver* and *Adder*, were stationed at Lowestoft to protect the fishing fleet. The loss of nets fell equally on fishermen and boat owners. All were losing money. Mr. H Fuller master of the *Leo*, W Smith of the *Surprise*, J Lewes of the *JJC*, W Catchpole of the *Eric* and J Ecclestone of the *Sunbeam*, were summoned to Ostend and gave evidence. Mr. J Mickleburgh, part owner of five fishing vessels, gave evidence to the effect that, but for the services rendered by the cruisers, the inhabitants of the fishing village of Pakefield would have been unable to shoot their nets, and would have been reduced to starvation in consequence.

By 1887, Pakefield Beach Company was unable to carry on, and was wound up. Although it was re-founded in 1890, with a new yawl, when the lifeboat was withdrawn in 1922 to be replaced by a motor boat in Lowestoft Harbour, the company closed for good. After this, the beach at Pakefield became focused on leisure. Bathing machines and bell tents began to take the place of the yawls, as Pakefield gradually became subsumed into the southern expanse of Lowestoft.

Kirkley Church and Water Tower, before housing development, and the late Victorian improvements to the church. The water tower was built in the 1850s to supply the new development of Kirkley with water. Kirkley Church stands in an oval enclosure, which is often an indication of a very early Christian enclosure, as is the parish name, "church meadow". Neolithic hand axes have been found nearby. For most of its history, Kirkley was very sparsely inhabited and was administered from Mutford. In Domesday there were nine families living in the parish, some of whom were involved in fishing. By 1327 it was listed with Pakefield, probably because most of the population had already gravitated to Pakefield Street. In 1676 Kirkley had only 106 inhabitants aged over sixteen, and the church could not be maintained. It was

abandoned about 1640, and the parishioners resorted to Pakefield Church. In 1736 the church was still in ruins. In 1748 it was decided to rebuild the church. Rev. Tanner of Lowestoft organised a substantial collection throughout Suffolk and Norfolk to fund the works. About a third of the cost was covered by selling the old bells of the church. It was thatched with reeds from Benacre and the font was purchased from Gillingham Church. Services recommenced in 1751. By 1845 Kirkley had 433 residents, whose occupations were predominately to do with farming. It was a typical, self sufficient rural village, with its butcher, draper, shoemaker, carpenters and bricklayers. Fishing and boatbuilding activities were evident, with coopers, sailmakers, shipwrights and fishermen also living there. While most people lived along Pakefield Street, a few had boat building works at Kirkley Hamm on Lake Lothing, and a number of houses and pubs had sprung up along London Road near Lowestoft.

A view from Kirkley St. Peters Church looking over the new development of Kirkley. The farm buildings in the foreground are in Carlton Road and were owned by William Everett in 1841. The farm was part of an estate that ran the whole length of the cliff between the Turnpike Road and the sea, down to Pakefield Street. The area opposite the farm was a field known as Catchpole's. Beyond this is land that was previously part of Kirkley Common. In the distance can be seen the old mill at Kirkley Hamm on Lake Lothing. This was described in 1813 as "a substantial and commodious freehold Tower Brick windmill with cottage, stable, granary, baking office, and a most excellent oven, lately erected at more than £200 expense." The miller, Bartholomew Barcham Last supplied bread for Lowestoft and also owned a freehold baking office in the High Street of Lowestoft. Kirkley was developed rapidly in the second half of the 19th century, as agricultural land was built on. Shortly after this photo was taken, the farm was demolished to make way for further housing. From 1841 to 1911 Kirkley expanded from a sparsely populated area of 433 inhabitants to a fairly densely populated town with many houses. The area depicted here was being planned in 1856, when maps were drawn up to build on the Kirkley fields, all the way from the harbour to Pakefield Street. This part became poor and populous, occupied mainly by workers on low pay.

By contrast, the seaside development was aimed at the wealthy and affluent. This was a key part of Sir Samuel Morton Peto's ambitions for Lowestoft: he would have a railway not only to carry away fish and imports from the Continent, but also to bring tourists, who would be able to stroll along the broad promenade and enjoy the golden sands. An 1845 Act of Parliament allowed him to build the north and south piers, which formed the harbour completed in 1848. The Esplanade, shown here, opened in 1849 and the Marine Parade, which overlooked the well-kept gardens at the rear of the Esplanade, was completed by 1851. Wellington Terrace, with its semipublic gardens, was finished in 1856. These new properties attracted a prosperous community including landowners, fund holders, gentry and lawyers. The opportunity to get work in the building and carpentry trades attracted people into the area from other parts of the country, and so did the prestige of owning a splendid property that overlooked the sea.

Lowestoft was renowned for its sun and absence of rain and was advertised as a health resort. Kirkley was deliberately developed as a leisure resort from the 1840s. In 1893 it was referred to as "the aristocratic quarter," and in 1919 observed to be "an airy suburb, with row upon row of stately houses and large hotels, the chosen haunt of the fashionable who, in palatial surroundings, live a life apart from the throng on the beach." Visitors came by train, or by boat. The parades and hotels built by Peto aimed to provide comfortable accommodation. In 1883, Clement Scott described Lowestoft as "the very pink of propriety, the cleanest, neatest and most orderly seaside spot at which I have ever cast anchor. It would take a chapter to enumerate the advantages of Lowestoft, whose friends seem never to desert it. It has public gardens of every kind, many opportunities for cricket, golf, and tennis, with a surrounding country of great beauty, from which you can get a peep at the broads." The sea wall was constructed but not yet any defences against the sea pounding the beach and cliff at Kirkley.

The 1861 census shows that people continued to move to Kirkley from other places and worked in a variety of trades needed by a growing population and a building programme. Wellington Parade, Marine Parade and London Road now had several lodging houses and there was a boarding school in Marine Parade. The Esplanade continued to attract well off clientele such as landed proprietors, a magistrate and a justice of the peace, whilst streets further from the sea such as Horn Hill, Union Street and Church Street provided homes for the working class. Farmland went up for sale and builders developed it into streets of houses. In April 1867 national newspapers advertised a Pakefield farm and a Kirkley farm for sale. It was not long before houses were built on them.

By 1871 Cliff Terrace was newly-built with five houses still unoccupied. The architect John Clemence lived in one, seven were owned by lodging house keepers, there was a professor of music, a clerk, and a custom house officer. Wellington Esplanade in the 1871 census shows five owners who were born in Middleton, Suffolk. In the boarding school three scholars from the Thornhill family had been born in India. In 1881 of the fifteen properties only one was unoccupied. None of the householders were born locally – places of birth being London, Suffolk, Norfolk, Northumberland, Worcester and Rangoon in Burma. The latter were the children of an army officer. On 29th August 1885 a charter united Kirkley with Lowestoft, making it one borough with a mayor and corporation. The first part of Kirkley Cliff Estate was built in 1887 with marine residences forming Cliff Terrace.

At the end of the Esplanade, near the harbour, was the Royal Hotel Towards the centre were a number of boarding houses such as Hatfield House, which in 1902 was owned by Mrs. Mary Ann Blackburn, and Victoria House next door. By 1926 Hatfield House Hotel (incorporating Seafield Hotel, which was next door, and had now been connected by a corridor), was owned by Mr. and Mrs. Henderson, and boasted, in addition to the magnificent sea views, "excellent and liberal cuisine and prompt service, excellent furnishings and equipment" including electric light throughout. It had public rooms, a large dining room (with "separate tables"), lounge, smoking room, writing and reading room, and a recreation room – all of which directly faced the sea.

This shows the clash of seaside cultures. To the left are the Olympian Gardens, "tastefully laid out" where in 1919, al fresco concerts were given twice daily, consisting of humorous songs, ballads, and instrumental music, varied by occasional quick changes and other artistes. In the foreground however are the wagons of various sellers and hawkers, a number of whom in August 1902 were prosecuted when Lowestoft Corporation introduced byelaws prohibiting such activities on the beach, even between the high and low tide marks. These wagons are lined up right on the edge of the corporation boundary, which ran down to Claremont Pier, so they could sell without breaking the law. Jonathan George, who was charged, angrily pointed out that he gave value for money with his sales, unlike the Salvation Army and other church ministers, who "cadged and begged" on the Esplanade, and why should he not offer his fruit on the beach – he had as much right as anyone else to be there, and fortune tellers weren't prohibited. He had to make a living. On being sentenced to a fine or serve 14 days instead, he replied "I'll take the days sir. The byelaws are rotten and ought to be rescinded, it's nothing but false imprisonment."

Henry John Cook, a missionary with the North Beach Bethel, led open air meetings in the district for 53 years, before dying on 28th May 1911 actually conducting a morning service in the Bethel. His last words were "he'll welcome his faithful home." This beach service is conducted by students of Cliff College a methodist training school in Derbyshire. For some, hearing an open air service could be life changing. For others, it was just part of the holiday routine. One person wrote home in August 1913 – "We had a good time yesterday. Went to the Sailors Bethel open air meeting in the fish market at 10 am, inside at quarter to 11. Open air on beach at 3pm and Baptist Chapel at 6.30pm and Open air at 8 pm."

Evangelistic conferences were held on the cliff top. One was the Church Mission Society summer school, held in May 1914 in a marquee in the grounds of Cliffside Private Hotel in Kirkley. This annual event, started in 1904 at Keswick, was designed to teach the members about the work of the CMS, founded in 1799 to carry out cross-cultural evangelism. In 1914 nearly 500 members came to the school.

A similar event was the annual "Pakefield Convention", held in the Rectory gardens for several years. There was at this time a significant growth in Christian belief in the Lowestoft area, as in 1921, following many years of prayer and missionary work, a 'revival' took place in which many hundreds of people turned to Jesus Christ during the preaching of such men as Archibald Brown from London, Jock Troup from Fraserburgh and fellow Scotsman Hugh Ferguson. The churches were packed and people had to sit on the windowsills. People were profoundly changed: whole fishing boat crews were converted, employers and employees dealt more honestly with each other and families that had fallen out were reunited.

These young men were known as Church Army Pilgrims and marched from Derby to Lowestoft for the purpose of holding a beach mission for five weeks in the summer. The Church Army was started by Wilson Carlile, curate of St. Mary Abbot, Kensington, who began a small evening open air service to appeal to servants who were finishing their duties but would be unwilling to attend a church service. He gradually built up a following of such people who joined in the singing, read passages from the Bible and gave testimonies and short five minute messages. Carlile then trained these working men as evangelists, and in 1882 the Church Army was born. Carlile spent much time working with the poor, in some of the worst slums in London, and there was some resistance from others in the Church of England to his methods. Carlile said, "*We do not seek to drag the Church of England into the mud but to bring some of the social mud into the church*". He was helped in his work by his sister Marie Carlile, who like him left a life of elegance, comfort and ease, for one of austerity, hard work and persecution, amongst drunkards, thieves and prostitutes. She superintended a Women's training college that was part of the first large scale opening for women workers in the Church. The Church Army worked hard to help the addicted and abused to find new life, offering homes for men and shelters for women, rehabilitation and training in useful skills. From 1892, Carlile also tried to reach out to the poor in rural districts as well and sent out mission vans to preach in the countryside. During the First World War, the Church Army operated recreation centres for the troops, hostels for the limbless, care for soldiers' children who were motherless, and training for demobbed men. Prison missions followed, and in 1920 the 'Marching Crusaders' were first sent off.

The Marching crusaders aimed to preach the Gospel in the 'highways and byways' of the land. On one occasion in the Midlands, a lady Church Army Missionary addressed 1,000 rowdy men waiting for a boxing match to start, on the theme of "the great fight of life", in which the battle is against the world, the flesh and the devil.

As more of Kirkley Cliffs became developed for holiday and leisure, in 1902, Claremont Pier was built in pitch pine, as a landing stage for Belle Steamers (which ran to 1939). In 1909, the *Jarrolds Handbook to Lowestoft* observed that although the pier was not yet completed (the green heart T-piece was only added in 1912), steamers still landed and embarked passengers for Yarmouth, Southwold, Felixstowe, Walton, Ipswich, Clacton, and London. A band played during the season, with high class concerts every weekday, and a sacred concert every Sunday. By 1914 Claremont Pier had become the chief centre for sea angling in Lowestoft and with its benches and shelters was considered to be the most comfortable fishing station in Britain. The main season for this was the autumn, and most days the pier would be lined on both sides with ladies and gentlemen winding up whiting, and enjoying the "constantly changing marine panorama" as the drifters bustled into the harbour with their own catches of herring. There were also many anglers who fished all night.

In 1919, the Claremont was the head quarters of the Lowestoft Swimming Club and was reserved for the use of bathers from 6.30 to 8.30am. Here we see swimmers diving off the T-junction of the pier, with Kirkley Cliff. In 1940 Royal Engineers blasted a hole in it to prevent its use as a landing base. After the war a bridge was built over the gap but the pier was so badly damaged it was abandoned. The pier was saved by the actor George Studd in 1949 who took it over. Despite heavy spending and rebuilding the pier was not profitable. In 1962 the T-piece, known as 'cod corner', was finally swept away.

In 1909 the Hotel Victoria was owned by Henry J Heron and contained 50 rooms. Telegrams to it could be addressed to "Breezes, Lowestoft" – giving an indication of the bracing position it enjoyed. It was open all year and by 1913 had "motor car and cycle accommodation". In 1924 it had spacious bedrooms, which had been newly decorated, "service and cuisine of the best," a large ball room, with sprung floor, and a fine orchestra. It made a point of advertising that it had a garage, which in 1924 indicates the sort of wealthy people who were going to stay there.

Hotels were opened all along the sea front. Norfolk House was advertised in the Lowestoft guide of 1913, as a boarding establishment, "near the new Claremont Pier, beach, and most places of interest and amusement. Magnificent sea view. Excellent cuisine. Moderate and inclusive terms, according to season and position of bedroom. Good sanitary Arrangements. Electric light throughout. Cycle Accommodation".

Goat carts and donkey rides were loved by both children and adults, children because it was a great treat, and the parents because they enjoyed watching their children having a happy holiday. Not everyone accepted these animals with pleasure. The same people who were annoyed by the more popular forms of entertainment were also angered by donkeys charging along the beach, and having to dodge out of their way.

An essential seaside entertainment has always been Punch and Judy, which in 1886 was on the South Beach, but moved in 1902 to children's corner next to the South Pier. In August 1932, during a show, Eva Wright, aged 7, of Surbiton got into difficulties in the sea. The Punch and Judy showman, Richard Songhurst, quickly paused the show, and still in his clothes swam out to save Eva, then went straight back to his show to carry on with the performance! After the Second World War, Franklin Spence was the Punch and Judy man for about 20 years. In 1977, "Professor Jingles" (Bryan Clarke), who had been inspired as a child to take up entertaining by watching Franklin Spence, took over, until 1999, when it became increasingly difficult to make a living from beach performances and he moved on to doing children's parties, fetes and similar events.

On May 11th 1901, a calm and sunny day, while hundreds of people were enjoying the beach, the 1856 schooner *Flown* of Sunderland suddenly exploded, flames enveloping it from the waterline to topmost spar. The mate, Samson Clark, told the story: "We were drifting slowly before a light southerly wind, and all five of us were on deck, I being at the wheel. Suddenly there was a fearful explosion, the hatches of the main hold being flung bodily into the air and flames and smoke bursting out. The Dane and the American [two of the crew] were hurled out to sea, and disappeared, while the captain's wife was blown overboard on the other side. The captain and I were at first stunned, but soon recovered, and, seizing a long rope, jumped overboard. After searching around for her he managed to secure his wife. For ten minutes we hung on to that rope, the ship blazing like a furnace, singeing our hair and scorching our faces. The flames had quickly taken entire possession of the whole schooner, and we heard the shrieks and wails of the cat and dog, who must have been roasted alive." The Lowestoft smack (on the left) was nearby, and sent a barge (far right) to pick up the survivors. The two missing crew were never found. The captain's wife was so badly burnt her face was nearly unrecogniseable. An inquiry by Captain Thompson for the Board of Trade, found that the ship had been carrying about 2,000 gallons of naptha in wooden barrels, which exploded because fumes escaping from them were ignited by the fire on which the crew were cooking their dinner. He found that the captain had ignored the warnings he had been given, and recommended that petrol should not be carried in wooden barrels, on a wooden ship, on which the crew light fires.

Kirkley was mainly developed as a residential district for workers. London Road was an old road that had run from Pakefield to Lowestoft since time immemorial and became busier with the development of the turnpike in 1799, which improved the road along the coast, so that the main London to Yarmouth road ran via Lowestoft rather than Beccles. This shows London Road South, Kirkley in 1891-2 with an election poster for Harry Foster, who was MP for Lowestoft between 1892 -1900.

London Road South, the tram lines being cleared of snow. Shops on the right are L.E. Grices haberdashery, drapery and children's outfitters, next door to a hair dressers advertising hair cutting, singeing and shampooing.

Running off London Road were the main residential streets, such as Grosvenor and Windsor Road, on land that had belonged to the Charity of the Kirkley Poor. In the 1860s the semi-detacheds did not sell as rapidly as expected and by 1881 only twelve houses had been completed and were occupied. People living in Grosvenor Road worked as carpenters, joiners, labourers or in fishing as master mariners, pilots or fish agents, There was also a schoolmistress, three retired sisters who had been governesses and a clerk. In 1892 building recommenced and a terrace of houses, on either side of the road was built. Within two years, 20 houses were sold.

Construction of houses at the corner of Windsor Road and London Road South in the 1890s with the workmen posing outside.

Clifton Road, showing the type of houses that were being built in what was regarded as a poor area. The majority of the people who lived in this area, together with St. Leonards Road, St. Georges Road and Colville Road were born locally. The residents worked in shops, the trades, or fishing.

St Matthew's Church was built in 1898, as an outpost of St. Peter's Kirkley. The building cost was raised by subscription which fell short, but Mr. E Kerrison Harvey sold some land he owned to make up the shortfall. It was a half-timbered structure, and seated 500 persons. In 1915, the church ceased to congregate, and the building was then used as a dance hall, the Metropole, until 1930. The Bishop of Norwich subsequently sold it for £1,000 to a Brethren church, who had been meeting in Lorne Hall, in Lorne Road since 1920. They occupied it in 1935. Known as 'Colville Hall' it remained in use until about 1998 and was demolished in 2007.

In June 1910 the local newspaper announced that "The Sunday School teachers and choir boys, to the number of 40, left St. Matthew's and paid their annual visit to Fritton Lake. The party left St. Matthew's in brakes and arrived at 4pm. Here a most tempting al fresco tea was provided and they spent 3 hours on the lake. A start for home was made at 8.15."

St. Matthew's Sunday School building at the end of Clifton Road.

This screen, described as having "well carved figures and a cross 7½ feet in height" was erected in 1887 in Kirkley Church at the behest of Edward Kerrison Harvey esq. to the memory of his wife. It was moved in 1899 to St. Matthew's Mission Church. The Brethren would have had no use for such decoration. Joe Becket, who attended as a child in the 1940s, recalls that inside the quiet, polished floored hall was a large clock which could be heard ticking loudly, breaking the silence of worshippers praying, or waiting for a hymn to be announced. Some one would call out a hymn number, and Joe's father Herbert would start to sing in a slow, loud tone leading the way until everyone else joined in. There was no organ. In the autumn fishing season the church was full of Scottish fishermen on Sundays.

One of the leading members of Colville Hall was Herbert Beckett (born 1914), seen here on his motorcycle, with his four children, Paul, Joe, Steven and Rachel. The family, together with his wife Myrtle, travelled about in this vehicle for many years. So shortsighted that he was not allowed to join the army during the war (instead he was, ironically enough, required to serve as a fire watcher), Herbert was known to take his glass eye out to rest it on the table after dinner. He continued to ride a motor bike until he ploughed into a post office van that had stopped to empty a letter box in the 1970s. He then took to riding a bicycle, following as closely behind Mrs. Beckett as he could, this being the easiest way for him to find his way along the road. He never let his partial blindness impede his daily activities, even when this meant that he lost the end of his finger while cutting wood in his shed. Unperturbed he picked the end up and taped it back on again. Part of the Brethren tradition was hospitality for visitors. In the summer months, holiday makers came from all over the country, bringing with them a letter of commendation from their own church. Mr. and Mrs. Beckett frequently hosted such visitors for Sunday lunch, and though not wealthy, the food on their table would always stretch a little further. They also made their own home brew – from parsnip, rhubarb, orange, plum, elderberry – which Arthur Jackson in his memoirs *Tales from a Country Practice* describes, with some exaggeration. According to his recollection Herbert (who he calls Herbert Allcock) said "we do not make it. The Lord does. All we do is gather the berries and squash them in a large jug, and then wait til the Lord has finished working on it. As soon as He's finished working, but not before, we bottle it up and then leave it for five years. The Lord takes a little time to make His best."

Herbert, who was a cobbler by trade, also reared chickens, bred fish, grew plants and kept bees in his large garden in Dell Road. Here he is guiding a swarm he has collected into a hive. He continued keeping bees until he died in June 1999: as the family gathered in the garden after the funeral, a huge swarm of them flew out of their hive, and swooped round the mourners' heads, before flying back again. Maybe this is why they say when someone dies you should "tell it to the bees".

The tradition of the Sunday School was carried on by the Brethren of Colville Hall, who had about 170 children attending before the war. Families included the Lockwoods, Fullers, Posners, Moores and Becketts. However, very few returned to the Sunday School after the war, and for a time the work languished. However, it was restarted by Walter Freeman from Ilford, who held a few weeknight meetings during his summer holidays in Pakefield, in order to recommence the Sunday School. Joseph Beckett recalls that, "In the early 1950s, the Sunday School treat was the highlight of their year. As many as three coach loads would go on a short ride to a field at Blundeston. Here we played games, and Mr. Arms, who had a sweet shop, would run across the field throwing sweets which we children fought over to pick up. This was followed by a tea laid out on trestles and the children sat down on forms to eat."

Continuing down Clifton Road, where it turns into Salisbury Road, there was a further small chapel known as Salisbury Road Mission Room. The "Friends" (Quakers), who had occupied a tiny chapel in Lorne Park Road, moved into this hall in 1899. It was made of corrugated iron, and in 1902 the Quakers of Pakefield paid £250 towards the building costs. The Kirkley Friends had been busy with the adult first day school work and were particularly keen to proclaim the Gospel "in the very centre of Ritualistic Kirkley", a reference to the High Anglican tastes of the parish church. They were supported in their work by Pakefield Congregational Chapel and Lowestoft Bethel. Services held in the mission hall were open to all with freedom to accept what they then heard. This freedom was taken too literally by two Kirkley lads who, in 1906, were charged on remand with stealing a contribution box and its contents of three shillings from the Mission. They were discharged with a caution. A similar establishment was Providence Chapel, which opened in St. John's Road on 27th September 1868, 'in brother Hobson's back yard.' A few years later, as the minute book records, 'The Lord laid it on his mind to build a new chapel, he having some land in the Lorne Park Estate, Kirkley.' Hobson gave the land, built the chapel at his own expense, and it opened on 19th June 1878. The chapel was essentially bankrolled by Mr. and Mrs. Hobson, and when they died in 1911, it struggled, closing in 1916.

Rosemary Fuller in the yard of her home in Salisbury Road, holding John Wilson with Muriel Wilson beside her (her niece and nephew). They are the children of her sister Joyce. In the background is her mother Beatrice Fuller, known as "Beaty".

Towards the turn of the 20th century, the area in south Kirkley became developed, with streets such as Kirkley Street being laid out. In the 17th century this was farm land and just prior to development it was covered with the strawberry beds and cabbage patches of Soons Nursery Garden. Land was sold to a builder in 1900 and plans were drawn up with the intention of the houses facing a new road to the south. When the road was made, however, it was decided to build the houses facing Kirkley Street instead.

The south part of Lowestoft did not have a park, but the area around Kirkley Fen, a damp and undeveloped area near Kirkley Street, remained a green space. However, it was not until the 1920s when it was bought by Mr. Powell of the Lion Press, Lorne Park Road, that it became a park as such. Visitors were charged 2d for entry, and inside they could enjoy the small menagerie (monkeys and a crocodile), rowing, fishing and ice creams.

The Lowestoft Wesleyan Methodists had a vision of building chapels in the suburbs and in October 1899 launched a scheme to build a new chapel and school in Kirkley. On 11 September 1902 the land at 275 London Road, which had been a corner shop, house, stabling and outbuildings belonging to Fred Payne, was bought for £1065. The church was then built on the site and opened on 21st January 1904. It continued in use until 1963, when it became unsuitable due to lack of space, and disrepair. The congregation moved to a new building on Carlton Road and London Road South.

St. Peter's Road around 1909. This was laid out, on land that had been the garden of Morris's farm, as a grand avenue to lead from London Road to Kirkley Church, and in the other direction, to the seaside, where slopes were created to give access to the beach. It was part of the ornamental, geometric planning of the clifftop estate, which contrasted with the higgledy piggledy lay out of the streets further inland. St. Peter's was substantially altered in the 1870s and 1880s by the Anglo-Catholic rectors, who rebuilt the nave, added a side chapel, the north aisle and the north porch.

London Road South, Kirkley, taken at the corner of Economy Road. The old cinema is the large building in the centre of the picture, behind the telegraph pole on the right.

From 1904 to 1931 trams connected north and south Lowestoft. The line ran all the way to Pakefield, where it terminated next to the Tramway Hotel. The little shop on the left belonged to Gladys Foreman.

No. 13 tram was built in 1904 as part of a second batch of fifteen trams. Nos 1 to 11, the first batch, were built in 1903. This one is at Pakefield showing Croydon Lodge (built in the 1870s), on the right in Pakefield Street. The advances in locomotion brought new opportunities to bring products to consumers' attention and agents arranged advertising space on the trams. When a tram was taken out of action for repairs advertisers often requested a refund.

In the 18th century the main route to Lowestoft, which the London coach used to travel, was along Pakefield Street (right fork). Then the turnpike road was cut out across fields to make a direct route (left fork): we know it as London Road.

As the 1920s progressed, trams became more expensive to run than petrol-driven buses. They were less flexible, running only on existing tram lines. In Pakefield in order to travel further south, you would have had to get off the tram at the Terminus, and embark on a bus such as this Guy BB. On 8th May 1931 the last tram returned to the shed in Rotterdam Road wearing a wreath of laurel and lilies and driven by Mr. N Rudd, who had been on the trams for their entire 28 years. The tram fleet had clocked up 8 million miles between them, and never had a fatality.

Building plots became available in Kirkley following the deaths of large landowners like James Cleveland, the Kirkley mill owner (d.1864) or James Peto (d.1898). Kirkley Park Estate and Acton Estate expanded the development of Kirkley even further and provided a wider range of house types. Large houses sprang up in London Road that were ideal for holiday lets and boarding houses.

Kirkley Cliff Estate developed along the cliff. Along this road were many large houses, hotels and guest houses. Opposite were allotments which were replaced by Kensington Gardens.

This photo is from the Easty family collection, showing their car in Kirkley Cliff Road waiting to take them out with friends. The Easty family lived in Kirkley Cliff in a house called St. Monica, having moved to Lowestoft from Croydon. Alfred Mortleman Easty was a lieutenant serving as a shipping intelligence officer in the Royal Navy Reserve in 1919.

Over the years the holiday residences spread south through Kirkley. Kingswear Private Hotel, facing the sea, was at 39 Kirkley Cliff Road. It was owned by Mrs. B Matthews in 1904, by John Crisp Poyser in 1913, and in 1914 by Mrs. L Meadows. By 1924 she had extended it to include a large dining room and dance hall (to the left of the building in the picture), and in 1936, it was described as having a ball room with sprung floor, "a delightful sun lounge" and accommodation for 100 guests.

In August 1909 Banner House Boarding Establishment entertained this house party from London. Banner House was established in 1900 in Kirkley Cliff Road, and was run by Isabel Maud Calcutt, Susannah Marcionni and George William Arthur Garrod (also known as Wallis Arthur), until July 1916, when Isabel Calcutt dropped out. In 1924, it was advertised possessing modern sanitation, four bathrooms, cycle accommodation, electric lighting throughout, drawing, smoking and children's rooms and a spacious new dining room – with separate tables! On 13th February 1947, Susannah Marcionni (also known as Dolly Blackmore) died, and in 1953 it was still under the direction of Wallis Arthur, with Chas Blackmore.

Marlborough Christian Hotel, at 54 Kirkley Cliff Road was built for Bishop JC Ryle as his retirement residence, known as Helmingham House. Throughout the summer months of the 1890s he had stayed at various addresses along Kirkley Cliff, and regularly signed the visitors book at Corton Church. In 1891 he was active in raising funds for the extension to Christ Church School. Ryle was an evangelical, having become a Christian while a student at Oxford. He had firm beliefs, but was earnest in his desire to maintain the unity of the Church, at a time when there was great division over rituals like facing east when praying, wearing surplices and so on. He was zealous for all members of the Church to be active in living out their faith, rather than exhibiting just a nominal faith, and decried the unwillingness of some clergy to modernise. Ryle retired in 1900, intending to move to Helmingham House (54 Kirkley Cliff, named after the place where he was rector in his youth), but his health failed. After staying for some days at 16 Kirkley Cliff, he moved into Helmingham House, but died there on 10th June 1900. By 1936 it was known as Kensington Private Hotel, and provided accommodation for over 60 guests, boasting a professional chef, "constant indoor entertainment", with dancing a regular feature, and trips to the Broads and other beautiful or historic places. It was rather far from the railway station however, so advertised that the hotel car met all trains.

Kirkley Cliff Road was opposite Kensington Gardens. In 1905 a lawn tennis club was formed and an annual tournament was held.

The Empire Hotel once owned the land that became Kensington Gardens. The land was sold to the council in 1914 for £3,800 and was used to grow vegetables to support the war effort. In 1920 local businessmen, Selwyn Humphrey and Arthur Tuttle, turned the land into a park to provide work for the unemployed. The new park was designed by the borough surveyor, Sydney Hobbs, its formal opening on 10 June 1922 was celebrated by a carnival.

A boating lake, using electrically powered craft, was added in 1933-4. In the lake is a statue of Peter Pan, put there in memory of Ebenezer Tuttle who had been a leading citizen in the town. He had lived opposite the park, in Holm View, Pakefield Road (which later became the Grand Hotel). Many older people have fond memories of the boating lake and recall the hum of the wires overhead. The boat is being captained by eight year old Joe Beckett.

The park had a Japanese tea house, rockeries, tennis courts and bowling greens, with an annual tournament for the blind.

The clifftop fields that became Kensington Gardens were where Kirkley Football Club played from 1886 – the year before Lowestoft Football Club began. This shows the Lowestoft team in 1925-26. From left to right, the back row are Frank Foster, Dick Brinson, J Carr, M Marjoram, R Colby [chocolate Colby], C Hayward. The front row are Fred Wigg, Charlie Hook, B Wallay, Jack Borritt, H Hall. Fred Wigg also played for Pakefield Harriers, whose pitch was Home Meadow, where the Pakefield water tower now stands. They played every Saturday morning, marking out the pitch with sand they collected from the beach with buckets before the game. Fred joined the Lowestoft team in 1921 and in 1926 signed up with Norwich as a professional.

Kirkley Cliff Road turns into Pakefield Road, where the village of Pakefield was expanding northwards. Also opposite Kensington Gardens, and close to Pakefield was Tusculum, a private hotel, advertised by the proprietors Mr. and Mrs. T Mortimer as "pleasantly situated in the best part of town". By 1953 the proprietors, Mr. and Mrs. Ernest Orm, charged six to seven and a half guineas for their "excellent catering, personal attention, uninterrupted sea views overlooking the bowling greens and tennis courts of Kensington Gardens and the free use of a beach chalet."

From 1948 to 1951, Peter Baker used to come to Tusculum with his family for their annual week's holiday. Peter's father, who was a pharmacist, came to visit his best friend "Skipper" Sanders, who was a pharmacist in Lowestoft. Peter remembers playing with the Sanders family on the beach, and being taken in his pram each morning down to the harbour. In this picture Peter is on a fairground train with his father near the South Pier.

Kensington Terrace in Pakefield Road, was built before 1881, and overlooked (to the left) Cliff House and Holm View – marine mansions erected at the south end of the Kirkley Cliff promenade. They were part of the development of the north side of Pakefield Street, that had been Blacksmith Field. They were occupied by middle class people with a servant apiece. At the end of the row is the Congregationalist Chapel, built in 1903.

The corner shop on the end of Kensington Terrace was 22a Pakefield Road, which was a later addition to the row and built between 1927 and 1930. It was recorded as a stationers and post office in the 1930 *Kelly's Directory* and was run by Misses Mitchell and Middleton. By 1932 it had been taken over by Ernest Spurgeon, whose name appeared on the shop front, and Mrs. Sarah Spurgeon a corsetiere.

South Cliff Congregational Church, Pakefield Road, later United Reformed Church, now St. Nicholas' Catholic Church (since 1995). The fellowship that met here began in 1884 when the London Road Congregational Church purchased the Kendal Road Schoolroom from the United Methodist Free Church as a meeting place for the South Cliff Congregational Church Fellowship. In 1898 the Suffolk Congregational Union decided to expand into South Lowestoft, and the South Cliff site was purchased and given to the London Road church by JJ Colman of Corton. The foundation stone was laid in May 1902, and the new church opened May 1903. One of the first ministers was Edward Brine, an evangelical who went on to found the Evangelical Fellopship of Congregational Churches in 1947.The Kendal Road schoolroom continued to be used as a Sunday School and for other activities, until 1959, when it was sold and the money used to extend the church hall in Morton Road. In 1972 the Congregationalists joined with the Presbyterians and the church became the South Cliff United Reformed Church and was part of the Lowestoft group of the URC until 1983, when South Cliff broke away. The London Road and Oulton Broad churches joined together to become the North Lowestoft United Reformed Church in 1983. The last service was held 30th July 1995 and the church buildings sold.

At the southern end of Kirkley, there was a group of large villas, developed for those wealthy residents who wanted to be away from the bustle of the main seaside resort. Clarendon House was built on the west side of Pakefield Road on the corner of Morton Road, between 1892 and 1901. After the Second World War it was one of the exciting empty old buildings that children used to clamber into and explore. It was demolished in the 1960s. Next door was "Chesterfield" House, previously known as Kendal Villa, which went on to become a childrens' home.

Opposite Clarendon House was Holm View, the 12 bedroom marine mansion of Captain W F Larkins JP, who was the pioneer of the International Code of Sea Signals, when in 1864 he was sent by the Board of Trade to Paris to devise this new system with the French. The work proved to be a great success and was used on all British, French and American vessels from then on.

After its sale in 1892 the villa was extended and became the Grand Hotel, opening on 10th July 1893, as "the best hotel on the east coast", with room for 120 guests. The proprietor was John Whaley, who also owned the Royal Hotel, Lowestoft and in London Woods' Hotel, Furnival's Inn and Ridler's Hotel, Holborn. He was an "experienced and always energetic hotel man" who kept a sharp eye on the cuisine and wine cellar, and realised the importance of amusing his guests. The Grand Hotel was the largest hotel on the East Coast, with 200 rooms and boasted a resident band during the season, ball room, tennis courts, bowling green and, new for 1936, the Grand Empire Hall, which was in the hotel grounds, offering conference seating for 2,500. In 1915 it was the head quarters of the London 25th Regiment, who were posted to the east coast for the year. On 6th September 1963, the Rolling Stones (without Brian Jones) played in the Grand Hotel Ballroom. Its charms were not appreciated by everyone. George Grossmith, entertainer and comedian, complained bitterly to his agent for booking him into the Grand: "What in the name of Thunder, Hell and Lightening did you send me to this hotel for? It is not in Lowestoft at all; miles from pier, public hall and railway station. I shall be ruined in cabs, to say nothing of the damned isolation. The Royal is surely the best place here. Make a note: this is something between a brand new workhouse, a school board and the Metropole, Brighton. Comfortable no doubt, but in the desert of Sahara."

A similar venture was the luxurious Empire Hotel, which was aimed at really wealthy visitors. Opened in June 1900, with 299 bedrooms, it boasted a banqueting room, minstrel gallery, billiards room, lounges, library and writing room, several small halls, about 20 grand pianos, lounges, a drawing room and an apartment decorated in the style of Louis XV. It was built by Spiers and Pond Ltd, who were at the time famous all over Europe and America for their catering. This firm had been founded by two Australian entrepreneurs, whose first ventures had been the Cafe de Paris Restaurant in Melbourne, and the catering on the Melbourne and Ballarat Railway. Given the great love Australians had even then for cricket, they decided to organise and sponsor a visit of English cricketers, which took place in 1862 and was the first Ashes tour. While in England organising this, Christopher Pond noticed the very poor quality catering for travellers, and he and Felix Spiers decided to move to England to change that. They started by opening a chop and steak buffet in Farringdon Station in London and continued to maintain connections with the railways, in particular by using the spaces under railway arches as restaurants, wine cellars and ice stores. After a few years, they contracted to supply refreshments for railway companies, and opened a series of hotels and restaurants in London, such as the Holborn, and the Criterion in Piccadilly Circus. They specialised in large scale catering (such as holding a huge party for 20,000 children in Hyde Park to celebrate Queen Victoria's Jubilee), and their UK business went on to include the Grand Metropole Hotel in Blackpool (which they also bought in 1900), grocery and wine merchandising, as well as the restaurant and dance hall that they developed in an unused railway terminus in Margate in 1863, and which went on to become the Margate Dreamland. By 1925, Spiers and Pond operated over 200 catering establishments in Britain.

The Empire at Lowestoft did not become a success though, and in 1921 had to close after just 21 years. It was soon taken over by the Metropolitan Asylum Board, under the name of St. Luke's Hospital (to reflect the Board's use of St. Luke on their seal and coat of arms). The refreshing sea air of Kirkley made it an ideal location for a TB sanatorium. The Metropolitan Asylum Board was founded in 1867 to provide for those in London who were sick and unable to afford medical care, who otherwise were at risk of death in workhouses. In 1911 with the National Insurance Act, it took on responsibility for treating TB for which purpose in 1922 it purchased the Empire Hotel to accommodate 200 surgical cases, with extra balconies built to be used as open air wards for sea air and sun treatment. In this picture the convalescents can be seen in their beds on both sides of the building.

Staff were permitted to play lawn tennis in the hospital garden. In July 1923 another tennis court was made available, in the newly opened Kensington Gardens.

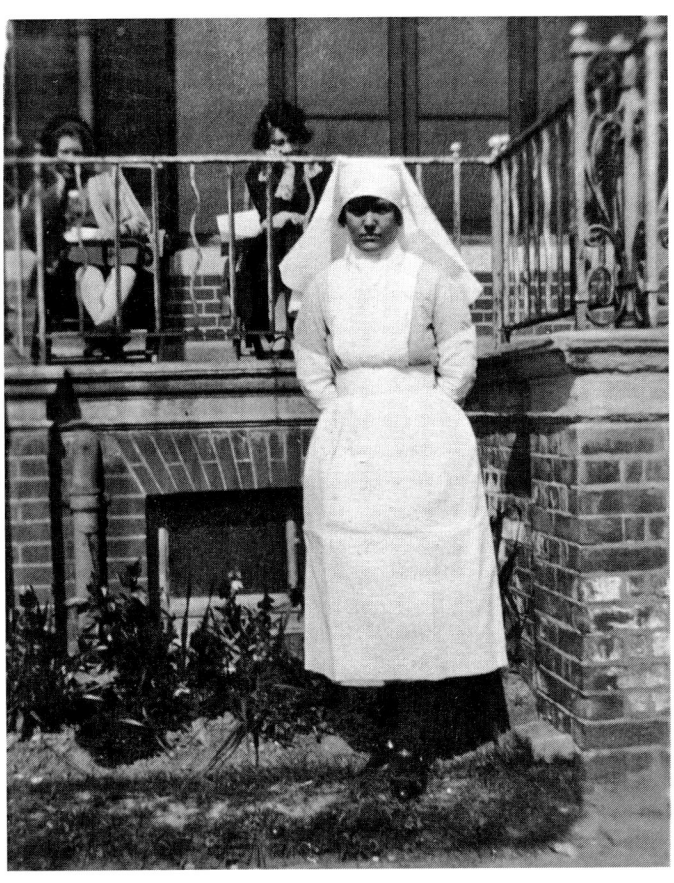

Nurse Ansdell in the hospital garden. Some patients are recovering on the balcony.

Eleanora Marion Campbell was appointed as a probationer nurse in December 1923 and passed her written and oral examination in the nursing of surgical tuberculosis. She received a certificate, issued by the Metropoitan Asylum Board, in September 1925, after completing two years training at St Luke's Hospital. She had many fond memories and there was always lots of fun. Her photos of patients and staff were taken between 1922 and 1927.

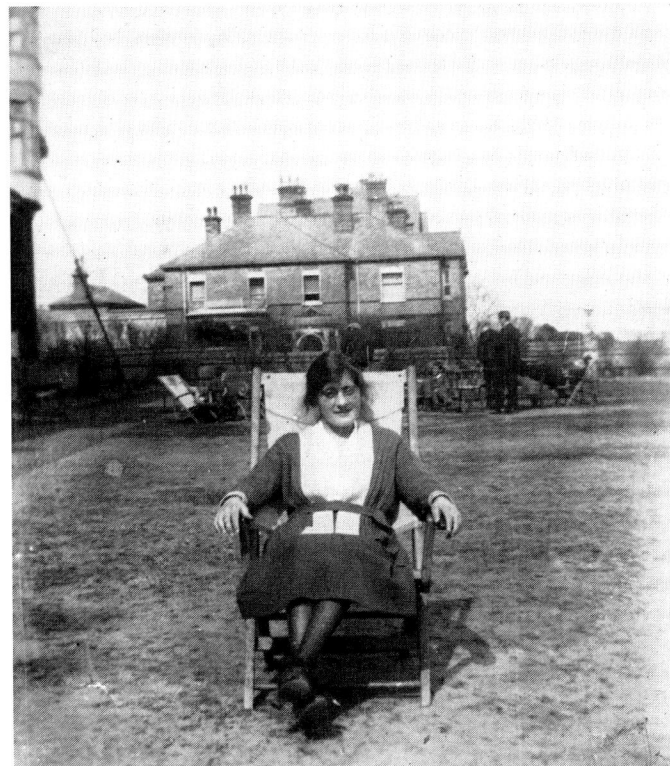

Lilly Stratford was knocked down and trampled on by a horse and the wound in her back became infected by TB.

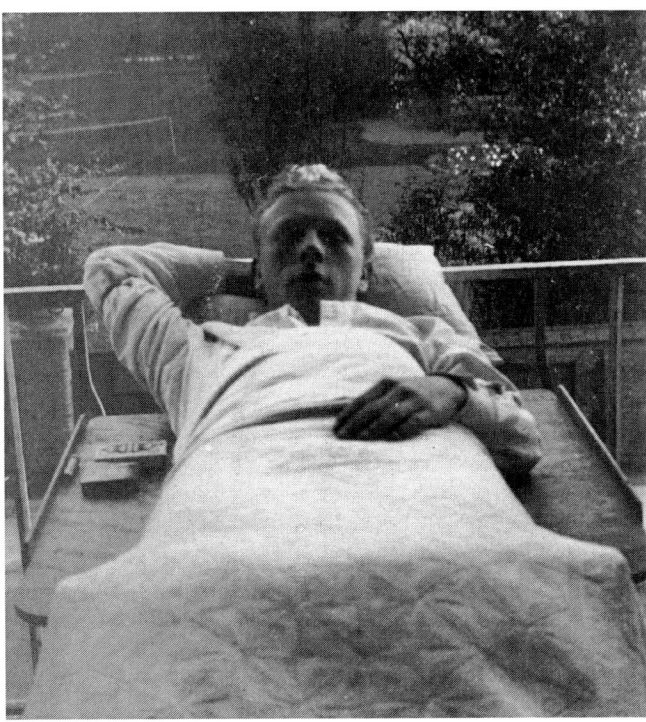

W Greenwood was one of those patients who had to stay in bed, but was able to enjoy the air and sunshine. Lowestoft has a reputation of not only being the most easterly point in Britain, but also receives the longest hours of sunshine in the country.

Wards D and E men. There were several patients who complained about the food. Bacon, fish and margarine seemed to be the main culprits. In September 1922 two staff left because they didn't like the food and didn't get enough. That December a patient from Greenwich also discharged himself. He said that the food was not good, he couldn't eat it, had lost 6 lbs weight and decided to go home. He said that all the patients would complain of the cooking and food if asked; and indeed they did. For in 1923 the patients nearly all signed a "round robin" complaining that the bacon was not fresh, there was not enough to go round and the fish had a peculiar smell. This was not surprising perhaps – one contract to supply fish was with a Grimsby firm, whose fish were far from fresh, and on one occasion 130lb of cod they supplied was condemned. It was too much also for Bertie Wiffin. He went home that year against hospital recommendation, writing about the food, " Some of it was good and some was impossible to eat. I know accidents happen but they seem to happen rather often there. We had kippers for breakfast. For dinner steak pudding and the forks tasted strongly of the fish from breakfast. We had tapioca pudding for second course, and that was cooked in the fish tin. Water too tasted of carbolic." The matter was looked into and the conclusion was that margarine was not liked by the patients, but would be improved by adding 10% of butter to it. The fish supplier should be changed as there was no doubt that fish was at its best if it was local.

"A Ward girls". These were staff who worked with Eleanora Campbell on that ward. They were a happy bunch and no doubt helped to keep up the morale of the patients and cheered them up. Indeed spirits sometimes were so high that one Boarding House keeper who lived in Rectory Road close by complained about the noise, so the hospital put up blinds to "prevent noise from patients."

The Sands at Pakefield.

Pakefield, due to its proximity to Lowestoft, also developed a holiday trade. It was described as "a favourite resort for those who need the pure, bracing air, and yet have no liking for the gaieties of the town." In 1936 it had three miles of firm yellow sand and tents on the beach. Just right for those who "prefer the natural quietness to the man made attractions of a large and flourishing seaside place". Pakefield is the place to go if you prefer a quiet holiday.

Summer 1928, Amy, Walter and baby Malcolm Freeman enjoying their holiday on Pakefield Beach. The knitted swimming costumes used to stretch to almost falling off when they got wet, so it's a good job they had a bathing machine to hurry into!

It was a time to relax, have fun and fool around, Bill Campbell, with brother-in-law Walter Freeman by a bathing chalet on Pakefield Beach, pretending to be "city slickers" on the beach – you're not properly dressed without a tie.

The fishing boats on Pakefield Beach in the 1930s – Edna Campbell of Glen Manna seated in the boat, with Malcolm Freeman and mother Amy Freeman.

As well as the Cliff Hotel, at the other end of Pakefield Street was the Tramway Hotel. This was probably named the Half Moon at first, then Crown and Anchor and was built in the 1880s on land that had been part of Mill Common. It was renamed the Tramway in 1904 when the Lowestoft tramline arrived. Opposite was a rival establishment known as the Prince of Wales.

Glen Manna was built in 1898, on land auctioned in 1897. George Elsey a builder, bought the land and built Glen Manna, Nelson Road, Wellington Road, Chapel Road and St. Georges Road Kirkley. George Jacobs, a butcher, lived there and kept his horse and wagon in the stables at the end of the garden, which had entry to Florence Road.

Left: London born Walter Freeman went to Lowestoft to work on the fish market as a fish buyer, to send fish home to his father, who was a fish salesman at Billingsgate Market. Walter got friendly with Jimmy Campbell, who was a fish merchant at Lowestoft fish market. Walter had lodgings in Windsor Road Kirkley and so when Jimmy invited him home to tea he readily accepted. Jimmy's intention was to show him his prize rose in the garden. Walter was delighted when he saw an even better prize rose, namely Jimmy's eldest daughter Amy. Romance blossomed and they got married at Pakefield Church, on 30th May 1925, and had their reception in Glen Manna garden.

Walter's fish business unfortunately did not survive the Depression, and he was left without work. Being enterprising he cycled round to look for employment. Arriving at Shell's head office, he asked to speak to the top man. He had to wait, but the manager was impressed with his initiative and took him on as a petrol salesman. This became a lifelong career that Walter loved, and excelled at. Here he is filling up his 1953 Standard Vanguard at the Shell petrol garage opposite Glen Manna. That car stayed in the family until it was sold off at auction in 2013.

"Fernside" was built about 1905. In 1938 it was occupied by Walter Woodgreaves, before 1910 a partner in the engineering firm of KWG Engineering Company of Belvedere Road, later a fish exporter. By 1948, the building was being used as a fire station. In 1957 it was again a private house, occupied by the Readhead family, before in 1965 becoming Pakefield Hotel. For a number of years it was run by Christopher and Sylvia Braggins. In 1973 it was taken over by Leonard and Mary Corby, before being demolished to make way for the Seventh Day Adventists Church (foundation stone laid 7th June 1974).

Built on land that was once a garden owned by Nathaniel Squires, and before 1799 was part of Mill Common, the Silver Poplars stood at the junction of Florence Road and Saxon Road, just outside the Cliftonville Estate. It was built in 1926, but has now been replaced by other houses. In the background to the left can be seen the roof of Fernside. The Cliftonville Estate, which covers much of Pakefield Parish today, was built with high hopes of turning Pakefield into a fashionable watering hole. While most of the inland streets remain, the whole of the cliff edge development, together with the fortunes of those who invested in it, has been lost to the sea.

The bungalow on the edge of Cliftonville Estate where Mr. Davies lived. In the distance is the Firs Hotel, next to which is one of the lifeboat houses built of brick. Mr. Davies senior purchased two large portions of land, which extended from Pakefield lighthouse to Pakefield Street. They were laid out into freehold building plots., and auctioned off by a London firm. Advertisements in the newspapers were enticing, describing the land as " being situate on the summit of Pakefield Cliff, 50 feet above the sea level. The land now offered commands magnificent views over the sea and surrounding picturesque country. It is admirably adapted for the erection of marine residences and shops, which are here in great demand." What speculative person could resist the opportunity of a day trip from London to Lowestoft, on a special train chartered for the event, with lunch thrown in, and the chance of buying a prime plot? Hundreds of people came and the sale of land was a great success. The first auction of part of Cliftonville Estate took place in September 1885, when 475 people attended from London. All 90 plots sold (ranging from £20 to £200 for ordinary building plots, with the "hotel" plot facing the sea and with ornamental gardens, selling for £1,320), and it was acclaimed the Sale of the Year. The second portion of 134 plots was auctioned in 1886, which included sites for marine residences and 46 shops. Again the auction was advertised in national papers, and potential buyers were given free return tickets from Liverpool Street. In the event over 150 people travelled on this train, and 20 waggonnettes were laid on to convey them in style along Marine Parade, Victoria Terrace, Wellington Esplanade and Kirkley Terrace, to the auction site. It was a particularly fine day, and the visitors were full of admiration for the views. At the Cliftonville Estate, in a marquee, a 'substantial lunch' of fowl, ham and beef, ale and champagne was laid on, followed by a stroll over the estate. Then at 3pm Mr. Baker, the auctioneer, reminded the gathered company of the chief attractions of Pakefield (including the low death rate!), and the sale began. Within an hour all the plots had sold. This was a fateful day for many investors, who paid between £18 to £87 for each building plot, with the hotel plot selling for £575.

The Firs was built by, Isaac Jones, a Devonshire man, who hoped to profit from the sunshine and sea at Pakefield, as well as its close proximity to Lowestoft, then the most fashionable watering hole on the east coast. It was about half a mile from Pakefield Street, and was on the cliff edge. He was living there in 1901 with his wife Jessie, daughter Jessie, and three little sons, Eric, George and Cedric. His investment and dreams were soon lost when the hotel went over the cliff a few years later. The shock and the stress seem to have been too much: Isaac was buried 6th January 1904, aged just 49.

The men who developed Kirkley were very optimistic. Looking across the fine sweep of sandy beaches they saw a sea that was their friend – a beguiling fascination that would attract tourists from far and wide, to fill their hotels and spend money in their restaurants. Hotels like the Grand, depicted here on the left, or the Empire in the middle distance they saw opportunity to improve the poor fishing village, and make money on the way. However the sea is a dangerous friend to make.

The people of Pakefield saw the success of the Kirkley beach resort, and determined to make the most of their cliff top vantage point. Beach huts, tents and bathing machines would attract those tourists who wanted a quieter style of holiday –with the authentic fishing community and lifeboat at hand. The views and bracing sea air would also attract those who wanted to work in or retire to the area, meaning that there was plenty of money to be made by those who owned land along the shore.

In 1891 the auction of 87 freehold building plots of Pakefield Cliff Garden Estate took place. Building plots sold from £16 to £46 according to the depth of the land. Some of the initial buildings, in Cliff Garden Road, can be seen on the right, with the houses of Church Road in the centre. Just as Kirkley had been developed with a grand building scheme, there were plans to turn Pakefield into a luxury watering hole. *Floods Guide* (1890s) extolled the "the enterprising spirit of Mr Davies of The Bungalow, locally, and London, the magnificent owner of the Cliftonville Estate" to whom "Pakefield owes much, and will owe yet more in the not distant future, when this magnificent building property is further developed. The sea wall, for the protection of the cliffs in the vicinity, has been constructed by Mr Davies at enormous expense, so as to contrive a double debt to pay. In addition to its acting as a protector from old Neptune's mad forays, the top of the wall forms a capital esplanade of very respectable width indeed, and of which outlying visitors in Pakefield will doubtless avail themselves to the utmost during the glorious days and nights of the impending season." Despite continual erosion, another hotel site (on The Drive) was auctioned in October 1893, and a further 17 plots along Pakefield Avenue and Cliff Gardens were auctioned on 16 August 1900!

Taken from Lifeboat House looks towards the church. The houses to the left of the Church are Alexandra Road. On the right is the short-lived Cliff Road (which ran off what is now All Saints Road). Where the beach is just in front of the garret windows is where Pakefield House was. It first appears on the 1881 census and was owned by William Hubbard, a 60 year old retired farmer from Lincolnshire, where he lived with his wife, two daughters and son, William, who was a farmer and brick maker employing eighteen men and five boys. According to the census it appears to have been unoccupied for the following 20 years, but his son William owned land on the estate by 1895. In November 1903 the *Lowestoft Journal* wrote of the shocking death of son William. He was found with a photograph of his wife and children in his pocket, together with a memorial card relating to the death of his mother, and a catalogue of a sale of furniture by Mr AG Notley on Oct 5th 1893. He had fallen on hard times.

One part of the Cliftonville Estate to survive. The Oddfellows Arms at 6 Alexandra Road was a successor to the pub named, first the Good Woman then the Morning Star, which was on the cliff, next to the beach men's huts. After it went into the sea, beer was sold from a temporary building, but then its licence was transferred here in August 1902. The pub had two rooms at the front, which were let out to lodgers, with room for the publican and his family at the rear.

On 3rd February 1791, the sea flooded with such violence into Lake Lothing, that it washed away Mutford Bridge and killed many of the freshwater fish; it also undermined the cliffs at Pakefield, "just at the instant that a poor old woman was holding on some paling near the precipice, when a large body of earth gave way and carried her down with it." She fell 40 feet, but remarkably was not hurt, and was able to regain the cliff when a ladder was lowered to her. In January 1793, a newspaper noted that the bad weather and "remarkable high tides" had flooded the turnpike road through Kirkley, and that the sea "continued to gain daily" on Pakefield. In 1812, a description of Pakefield noted that the ocean "is constantly dashing against the base of these cliffs, frequently undermining them, and has often received large portions of their ponderous masses, together with the buildings they supported, into its voracious bosom. Indeed, the town has so much decreased of late years by the rapid encroachment of the sea, that it may be fairly concluded, in half a century more, there will scarcely be a vestige of it remaining." The same guide observed that the cliff falls often revealed ancient coins, fossils and extraordinary large bones.

In 1844, Whites Suffolk observed that since the 1820s, 70 acres of Pakefield land, and several houses had been washed away. In January 1855 the cliff path was washed away. In 1815, 5 year old Maria Smyth was sitting on the beach at Pakefield, when the cliff gave way, buried her, and she was suffocated. On 16 May 1885, a cow belonging to a Mr Andrews of Gisleham was feeding near the cliff edge at Pakefield and fell 70 feet over the cliff. However, it got up and walked home, a distance of nearly a mile, apparently little the worse for the fall. The erosion seems to have increased in severity after the 1840s, and the causes were examined in a Royal Commission inquiry in 1906-1911. It seems that the erosion of sandbanks opposite Pakefield (on which people in the 1850s could picnic at low tide), and the shifting of the Pakefield Gat northwards, meant that the cliffs felt the full force of the North Sea. However, the building of the Lowestoft Harbour arms in the 1840s, and then Claremont Pier in 1903, is likely to have exacerbated the scour.

Here on the left are houses in Church Road (roughly where the All Saints Road car park is) together with the garret windows of Cliff Road –the furthest house has already been demolished, leaving only three garrets. In the 1880s, most of Pakefield village green went into the sea. 1892 *Floods Guide* refers to Pakefield "With its dizzy, sea-undermined cliffs and genuine old English village green". In December 1894, and then in January 1895, there were high tides of over 9ft, which tore into the cliffs, and stripped away the beach. Property owners tried to protect their land –this low concrete wall was erected by Mr Hubbard, who owned the Cliftonville Estate, in front of his lands from Arbor Lane to near Pakefield Street. He did not, however, put in any groynes, and like the other assorted sea defences tried by individuals (such as placing faggots in the sand or planting marram grass) the walls were entirely ineffective. The sea simply washed over them, attacked the cliffs and washed the walls away. A concrete wall erected in 1884 was washed down in 1895, and other works in 1896.

Opposite the Manor House seen in this picture, had been houses, such as that occupied by Walter and Susan Thompson, who between 1891 and 1901 had to leave their cottage and move to the newly built "Rugby Villa" in London Road, near to the Glendower Building –about as far away from the cliffs as you could get at the time without actually leaving Pakefield. The wealthier landowners, whose property ran up to the cliffs, were expected to defend their own land: Pakefield Parish Council did not have the funds to help, and other local authorities (such as Mutford and Lothingland Rural District Council) would not help, since the inland parishes didn't want to pay to protect other peoples' private property. And despite its territory running to Pakefield Street, Lowestoft Council would not help either –since Pakefield was at that time self governing. The result was piecemeal attempts such as this concrete casing built by Mr Thompson Hudson, who owned Pakefield Manor House, to protect his home. It too was completely ineffective, soon falling into the sea to become a local feature known as the Pakefield Rocks. In 1902 Pakefield Council considered whether to build groynes to protect the cliffs, but resolved "that as the whole of the sea front at Pakefield is private property, this council have no observations to make." The failure of Pakefield Parish to take collective action to defend the cliffs was to prove disastrous.

The threat to Kirkley was perhaps even greater. Here Peto's seaside development teetered on cliffs constantly at risk of being undermined. Individual landowners also built concrete casings, such as this in front of The Grand Hotel, but the sea, scouring the beach away, undermined all such efforts. Unlike Pakefield, the Corporation of Lowestoft spent considerable sums in protecting the cliffs with walls and groynes. Not all of these were successful, and in 1902 Nicholas Everitt evaluated their efforts and considered that they had spent many thousands of pounds on "totally inadequate" groynes. Towards the end of March 1898, a storm washed so much sand from Kirkley beach, that it dropped 5 feet, revealing old pipes, wells and drainage works. The waves were so powerful that they almost destroyed a "well arranged lavatory" built on a solid concrete base at the end of Claremont Road

He contrasted the efforts of Mr. JJ Colman who spent £100,000 defending Clyffe House, Corton to good effect, following the advice of the best experts obtainable, with the attempts of Lowestoft Corporation who have been "penny wise and pound foolish by following an altogether futile course of parsimony by experimenting in all sorts of fads and fancies, which the sea has swept away". Of the £11,500 worth of sea defences Lowestoft had built in 1900, Everitt observed most of them had been destroyed in the storms of March 1901 and the remainder were "practically doomed." Indeed records show that for many years, Lowestoft was spending at least £1,000 per year on sea defences and still the beach kept losing ground to the sea.

Part of Pakefield's problem was that it was just outside the boundary of Lowestoft, and the defences built by the Corporation tended to increase the scour into Pakefield. The piecemeal concrete casings and faggots thrown up by Pakefield landowners were simply washed away. This is illustrated powerfully by this 1901 scene, where it can be seen that the groyne being extended into the sea, at the end of Pakefield Street, in order to cause the beach to build up at Kirkley, has caused the sea to bite deeply into the land to the south destroying the concrete casing protecting the Manor House. The remains of the casing can be seen at the foot of the cliff. The situation was not helped by the practice of carting shingle off the beach for sale.

In November 1901 the fence near the cliff (put up only in August 1901) was carried away by storms, and the end of Pakefield Street had to be closed. The storms also washed away the lawn of Pakefield Rectory, on which Rev. Price held the Pakefield Convention. It was considered that the Rectory, built in 1861 next to High Bank House on the cliff top, was now uninhabitable. A campaign was launched in November 1902 to fund the purchase of alternative accommodation for the Rector. Money came in, and in 1903 a new Rectory was constructed in the Causeway. As it happened, the erosion of this part of the cliff slowed, and the clifftop rectory continued to be inhabited –being occupied in 1913 by a Miss Brown, who had moved in in 1905. Indeed in 1908, the cliff top rectory was valued at £200, and was sold by the Rector.

The Rectory on the Causeway. Rev. Sall moved in in July 1904, and marked the occasion with a house warming bazaar, to support the building fund, during which visitors could view the house, buy items and be entertained by a band on the lawn. Happily the new rectory has so far survived, and the rector was soon able to hold the Pakefield Convention, 'for the deepening of Spiritual life,' on its lawn again.

January 1903 The Lord Nelson pub, on the left and William Colby's house on the right.

Between January and April 1903, the cliff where Pakefield Green had been steadily eroded, taking the houses one by one. The Lord Nelson Pub is being demolished here, and William Colby's house (to the left) has already been taken down. The licence was removed to the "Lord Nelson" 333 Victoria Road. The building on the left in the distance is Pakefield House owned by Mr. Moffat.

Lowestoft Journal – APRIL 1903

"For some time now the cliff has been gradually going, but on Sunday night or early Monday morning a large portion of the cliff collapsed near the Lord Nelson, and carried with it a man hole of the Pakefield sewer, and smashing the water company's pipe which supplies this part of Pakefield. The water rushed out of the mains and further scored away the cliff. Information was quickly sent to the company's office, and Mr George Chaston [superintendent] and a number of men were soon at work. The pipe of course was useless, but a length of lead piping was led from Pakefield Street through the ship yard, and the residents thus continued to be supplied with water. The Lord Nelson public house, which was not long ago stood well back, it is now right on the edge of the cliff, and is so dangerous it is considered that it should be demolished."

A scheme of seven groynes was started in 1900 and paid for by Mr Moffatt, the owner of the Cliftonville Estate and Pakefield House, to defend his land. They were built by a Mr. Douglas of London, for £300 each. He offered that for a further £100 per groyne, he would guarantee that they would save the cliffs –and if not all of the money would be returned. However Mr. Moffatt considered that "if it is good enough for Mr. Douglas to guarantee, I think we may as well save our £700," and declined to take up the guarantee. This proved to be a mistake. Mr. Douglas was also advising the Lowestoft Corporation, and the huge groyne that he built for them at the end of Pakefield Street was so much bigger that it caused all the shingle in front of Pakefield to disappear, and by 1906 Pakefield lost 140 feet of cliff. In order to stop the scour, Pakefield needed longer groynes to catch the shingle as it headed south. However, Mr. Moffat who had by then lost Pakefield House, worth £2,000, as well as the £2,100 spent on groynes, decided to do no more.

The southern groyne being built.

This scene taken in November 1903 shows extensive damage to Kirkley Cliff, as well as the works to defend it. The correspondent who sent this postcard observed, "We could get no further than the pier as you will see by this view of the damage The sea came right over the pier on Thursday, we did enjoy it, felt the spray on our face." The posts in the beach are a revetment laid down in 1903 and made of a double row of piles filled with 3 inch horizontal planking. These were successful helping the beach to build up, but failed to protect the cliffs in high tide. They were exposed once more between the South Pier and Claremont Pier, by the 2013 storms which have stripped a significant amount of beach away.

The same scene in 1903 looking south. The groynes are those built by Lowestoft on the advice of Mr Douglas.

The house on the right is in Pakefield Street, running left are those along The Cliff, and on the far left are those in The Avenue – a short-lived development that was laid out off what is now All Saints Road. By 1906 the Manor House of Pakefield was gone. The revetment depicted was a further contribution by Lowestoft Corporation, which was effective at defending the northern side of Pakefield Street, but exacerbated the scour to the south. This wooden revetment was the latest to protect the cliff at the foot of Pakefield Street. In a series of attempts to halt the erosion –this was intended to catch the shingle and other debris, to stop it drifting out to sea. Built in 1903, it could withstand even abnormal high tides, and allowed the beach to build up. However, waves did go over it and scoured the cliff base. More significantly it covered only a very short stretch of cliff, so that other areas of cliff – especially to the south – were highly vulnerable to erosion. It was also a bone of contention with Pakefield, whose council in Oct 1905 passed the resolution that it "regrets that it can't agree to the erection of the revetment proposed by Lowestoft Corporation as it is convinced it will very seriously injure property in Pakefield – but it would consent to one continued in a straight line similar to the one in front of Pakefield Rectory."

The rows of faggots placed along the beach by Lowestoft Corporation, singularly failing to prevent the collapse of the cliffs at Kirkley during the high tides of 1905.

The sea came furiously onto the esplanade wall. Further along the rows of faggots apparently worked well, but at the southern end of them the esplanade wall collapsed due to the persistent sucking of the waves.

South of the harbour, there was serious flooding. The water topped the south quay heading, which it was considered ought to be heightened, and in a short time St. John's Road and Belvedere Road were submerged, along with a long stretch of London Road southward from St. John's Church. A tramgoing through dashed water against Hildyard House and some of it entered the hall. Photographers were in legions snapping everywhere, Mr Jenkins and Mr Metcalf were said to have secured good pictures, and were selling them at 2d each.

The 1905 storms prompted Lowestoft Corporation to redouble their efforts with sea defences, so in March 1905 they applied for a loan of £850 to build a timber revetment at the foot of the cliffs. The revetment at Kirkley Beach – was designed to stand sufficiently high above the beach level to protect the cliffs from abnormal high tides. It would be filled in behind it, so that the esplanade could be widened.

In the end, the Corporation decided to build a thick sloping lining of concrete to stop the sea scouring the soft cliffs. At the same time, concrete walls were laid down to the north of the harbour as well as to the south, at a cost of £68,000. The building of the Claremont Pier in 1903, being 760 feet long and 35 feet wide, is likely to have contributed to the build up of the beach to the north, but also to the destruction of Pakefield to the south.

The sea wall during construction. While the sea defences may have impeded people's use of the beach, they were successful in reversing the encroachment of the sea. Indeed the town clerk, Mr. Nicholson was appointed to the Royal Commission on Coast Erosion, due to his great knowledge on the subject. Lowestoft Corporation was so proud of its efforts that they invited journalists from all over England to stay at the Empire Hotel, and admire the sea defences, parks, bowling greens etc on the sea front. *The Tribune* reported on 9th July 1906 that "south of the harbour sand is banking up rapidly and at low water is a magnificent amount", and the *Manchester Evening News* on 11th July 1906 observed that the £68,000 sea wall had completely overcome the danger of further subsidence, and the sandy shore was in many places 12 feet higher than it had been in 1901. Both promenades and sea defences in position, the Corporation was determined that the Kirkley Cliffs would not be undermined. By 1913 the beach in front of Kirkley was building up, defended by ever lengthening groynes. While this was good for Lowestoft's tourist trade, it was disastrous for Pakefield. Which did not have the money to spend on substantial sea defences.

Looking down Pakefield Street, with the boats in front of Pakefield Green. The cliffs remained undefended in 1905, and houses were demolished, leaving spaces in the rows. The properties as far as the white houses were either pulled down or fell down with the cliff erosion. This is taken from in front of the Cliff Hotel, which six years previously had a 'nice garden and a big stretch of greenward in front on the opposite side of the road, is now not more than 40 feet from the edge of the cliff.' The Cliff (the houses to the left of the picture) was gradually eroding. Behind it was Stone Alley, which first appeared as that name on the 1861 census and had gone by the 1905 map. The wall of the Quaker church yard still shows where the plots of land ran to. The destruction of Pakefield was a curiosity for tourists, many hundreds of whom came to see the damage, but it was a sad business for the residents.

October 1905, Pakefield Street, showing a horse and cart loaded with possessions near the Ship Inn on the right. By this time people had to just empty their houses, demolish them if they could, and move away from the cliff edge. People were desperate to demolish and remove as much as they could because the high tides that began on 1st October 1905 were threatening the street.

A message on a postcard sent 12th October 1905 said "Perhaps you have heard of recent destruction at Pakefield. Nearly all the green has gone. The old houses are now demolished." To the south of Pakefield Street, what remained of The Cliff and the Cliff Hotel were edging ever closer to destruction. The flight of steps down to the beach dangling precariously away from the cliff, with the ruins of Mr. Hubbard's defences for the Manor House scattered across the beach.

With Pakefield being demolished around it, the Cliff Hotel bravely carried on business as the cliff came ever closer.

Its windows were removed and boarded up, but it continued to be patronised by some loyal customers.

On 17th March 1909, it was reported that the licence of the Cliff Hotel had finally been transferred to another site – the Carlton Hotel, London Road. In the background are the houses along The Cliff.

People had no choice but to demolish their own recently built houses to save what little they could from the catastrophe.

By the time this picture was taken, not many of the houses along the Cliff were left. Houses that had recently been built as part of the Cliff Gardens Estate had to be demolished. One of the victims of this disaster was William H Rice, builder, of Lanham House, Pakefield, who was bankrupted. He had built £17,000 worth of houses and they were all washed away or rendered unsaleable. He would have made £200 profit each but for the sea.

Demolishing buildings could be a dangerous undertaking. In March 1916 for example, James King, a 35 year old builder's labourer was pulling down a bungalow on the edge of Pakefield Cliffs, working at the corner of a wall 9 inches thick and 9 feet high, when he knocked some bricks away from the bottom of the wall, it was undermined and fell on top of him. Some soldiers came to help remove the debris and drag him from the wreckage.

In stark contrast with the many thousands spent by Lowestoft Corporation, in 1906, the Pakefield Committee passed a resolution recommending that the Mutford and Lothingland Rural District Council should spend £30 on Pakefield Beach for faggots for the protection of the foreshore. Even this was opposed by the district councillors representing Corton who said:- "We have had a good deal of sea erosion at Corton and if you are going to spend money at Pakefield we shall expect to have money spent at Corton." The chairman, Mr. K Rix, later said that "the view I took of that matter to spend £30 in faggots, was that it was just drifting into a scheme of sea defence that we did not know where we should end, and if we once began, as RD councillors, to spend a little trifle like that we should not be able to leave off." So no money was spent on Pakefield, and the erosion continued. At the Royal Commission which considered the issue from 1906 to 1911, Mr Rix felt that something had to be done, as the erosion would eventually turn Kirkley into an island, but it would cost about £20,000 to defend Pakefield properly, which the Parish Council would never be able to raise.

In May 1907 the Parish Council continued to be concerned about the revetment at the end of Pakefield Street, which they considered threatened the destruction of the whole village, and in October 1907 they formally requested that in view of the damage done by it, Lowestoft Corporation should formally consider incorporating the urban portion of Pakefield within Lowestoft in order to protect the village from the sea. The reply they received from the Lowestoft town clerk was, however, that "the application of your council cannot be entertained."

'Flea and Bug Row' on the left, just beyond the Jolly Sailors –lived in until 1908. Nos. 1 to 4 known as Sidney Cottages, were conveyed by Mr Harrison to Mrs Harrison in 1906, with a right to use the "Muck Bin" in the adjoining property ,once belonging to Edmund Colby, and paying part of the expenses of its upkeep. By now the Cliff Hotel had been demolished. The notice on the wall of the small house says "Photo Postcards of Collapsed Cliffs 2d". The erosion was not so rapid here, and the cottages were still standing in 1925 when they were sold for 10 shillings each, and were dismantled for rebuilding. In April 1909 it was reported "10 shillings is not an extravagant sum for a decent sized cottage and a garden, but that was the highest bid offered at an auction at Pakefield, near Lowestoft, the other day. There was certainly a slight drawback to the property. It was situated upon the edge of a cliff which for years past has been gradually eaten away by the sea, and it looks as though the next mouthful the wild waves will get is this cottage and the garden. When a cottage gets down among the breakers in a storm its value as a residential concern is not great."

The view along the cliff side of Pakefield Street in January 1909. One of the properties to the right in this picture was bought by a Mr. King in February 1902 for £95. Mr. King got about half his money back in rent before the cottage went into the sea. The building towards the left with two chimney stacks, one with five pots, is Pakefield Stores. A ramp has been built at the end of Pakefield Street to allow access to the beach. Since 1903 property worth about £600 in rateable value had been lost, with an average of 22 feet per year being eroded. Since 1900, 12 acres of land had gone. In November 1909, after further storms, James Norman of the Ship Inn, Pakefield Street was summoned to court for non payment of rates amounting to £6 15s 8d. In reply he said he had lost his customers and was doing no business. His house wasn't safe to live in and his shed had gone into the sea and the back approach to the house was washed away. His case was adjourned since he expected to have a reduction in the assessment!

Rider Haggard, the author, lived in this large house, at Kessingland, just along the cliff from Pakefield, and was one of the panel who interviewed and asked questions for the Royal Commission on coast erosion in 1906-7. There was concern that if Pakefield were to be protected with groynes, that it would cause a scour to the south and thus damage Kessingland. This view of Kessingland Grange, perching on the cliff edge, raises the question of if he was able to be unbiased towards the plight of the poor Pakefield people. By the early 1950s the cliff had erroded to the point that the Grange had to be demolished.

This house is at the end of Beach Street, which was fenced off for safety. This row of houses gradually fell into the sea over the following years. "On Saturday while the storm was at its height, thousands of tons of cliffs were demolished by the huge breakers bringing down the houses that stood near the edge of the cliff, which had been vacated some time previously owing to their dangerous position. One family whose back door opened practically onto the edge of the cliff, were compelled to effect a hurried removal, and were accommodated for the night by a kindly neighbour. Another house occupied by Mr Phillips and family had some 12 yards of the cliff at the back washed away during Saturday night and the family removed to Pakefield Street Sunday. The adjoining house is also apparently doomed there is only about 3 yards between the back door and the edge of the cliff, and one of the inmates we understand is lying dangerously ill, and could scarcely be removed if need be. The outlook generally at Pakefield is most distressing and the Parish council authorities and others appear absolutely helpless to provide anything by way of sea defence works. Pakefield is surely a case where the recent Coast Erosion Commissioner might have stretched a point in favour of the granting of some national assistance. During Sunday workmen were busy dismantling a house in order to remove a wooden building from the back yard. Mr Wright of Pakefield Street was also engaged in recovering part of his vinery, which was projecting over the cliff. Many townspeople visited the scene of destruction at Pakefield on Monday. The loss of cliffs must have been enormous extending for more than a mile in the direction of Kessingland. There are also huge gaps in the cliffs at certain places showing that many thousands of tons must have been swept clean away during Saturday and Sunday. In the opinion of several of the older inhabitants this is the most serious damage incurred within the past 14 years."

As Britain prepared for confrontation with Germany, in July 1913 the government decided to open a rifle range on the Pakefield cliffs. The two butts are visible on the far left of this picture. In many ways for obvious reasons an ideal spot, the bye-laws to be put in place under the Military Lands Act aroused considerable local opposition, with 171 boat owners, fishermen and beach men from Pakefield signing a petition for them to be changed. The laws aimed to stop people sailing in the firing line, by fining anyone there £5. However the area of sea over which the range looked was one of the best fishing grounds in the district, and as Rev Sall of Pakefield pointed out, this fine could be in addition to a fisherman being shot. He suggested that instead the fishermen should be allowed to continue to use the area, and instead receive compensation if shot! Some of the earliest units to camp at the range were the 450 men of the 6th Cyclist Battalion, Suffolk Regiment, who stayed from 25 July to 8th August 1914, the 300 men of the 6th Battalion Norfolk Regiment and 120 men of the East Anglia Supply and Transport Coy ASC.

Lowestoft Harbour had for some decades served as a naval port. This picture, taken in 1910, shows a destroyer being fuelled in Lowestoft Harbour. The arrival of new vessels was a source of interest, with the *Lowestoft Journal* reporting on 20th June 1914, for example, the arrival of the four torpedo boat destroyers, the *Quail*, *Success*, *Wolk* and *Lively* – "long black, vicious looking craft", which came into the South Roads and were viewed with interest by the considerable number of visitors. They went to the Inner Harbour and joined HMS *Halcyon*, *Speedy* and *Esther* – it was "like a little Portsmouth" as one onlooker put it. These naval vessels were stationed here largely to protect the fishing grounds, and to take appropriate action in the event of foreign boats being caught in British waters –such as when on 27th June 1914 HMS *Speedy* found a Belgian boat, O 950, fishing within the 3 mile limit off Kessingland, so took it prisoner and towed it into Lowestoft Harbour.

Alfred Mortleman Eastty, [in the front], lived at St. Monicas, 46, Kirkley Cliff Road, Kirkley. On 21st June 1915 Sub Lieutenant Eastty joined HMS *Mantua*, a British Home Waters armed merchant cruiser based in Glasgow, from barracks. He took his turn in being Officer of the Day and also of being in charge of a small boat and of boarding and challenging vessels at sea. The *Mantua* looked out for shipping and intercepted, challenged and boarded them, checking their paper work and taking prisoners to their own ship before landing them at ports. On 23rd August 1915, a German prisoner who had been taken to their ship was later taken under escort and landed at Lerwick. On 30th September 1915 the *Mantua* intercepted and boarded the Swedish Steam Ship *Avesta*. A few minutes later the boat left Sub Lieutenant Eastty in charge of armed guard. It appears that "While the armed guard was on board the *Avesta* on 1 October at 6.45am a German submarine was sighted. The *Avesta* hoisted Swedish colours and Sub Lieutenant Eastty ordered the armed guard to keep out of sight and hide their uniforms. He himself removed his naval cap and jacket and instructed the master to hide the guard and make no mention of their presence if stopped. In order to explain the *Avesta*'s position and course he was to say that the ship was proceeding into Kirkwall voluntarily. Unfortunately the *Avesta* had a German crew member who could not be relied upon to stay quiet so in the event it was decided to initially ignore the U-boat's stop signal and the *Avesta* maintained course and speed. Before the situation could escalate smoke was sighted on the horizon. Both parties assumed this to be another 10th Cruiser Squadron ship and the U-boat retreated. In fact the ship proved to be the American oil-tanker *Polarine* bound west across the Atlantic. The *Avesta* arrived safely in Kirkwall 18 hours later where the German crew member was handed over". (Ref: *The Big Blockade*, E Keble Chatterton 1932) Following this incident Alfred Mortleman Eastty was offered a Commission, on 6th October 1915, which he accepted. He retired by 1925 a Lieutenant Commander, and was still on the Naval Reserve list in 1940.

Soon after Belgium was invaded by the Germans, refugees began to pour across the sea in these boats, and found safety in Lowestoft. Many of these were fishermen and their families. Their plight evoked the sympathy of many Lowestoft people who went to the harbour to meet them and give them help. In the years before the war, the Lowestoft fishing fleet had suffered at the hands of the Belgians, who had often sabotaged their nets, but the people of Lowestoft were prepared to put this behind them at this time of need. Many of the Belgian fishermen remained at Lowestoft through the war, with 51 boats being based there in 1917.

As the war progressed, the German navy adopted the practice of attacking the UK's fishing fleet, on the basis that the whole North Sea was a war zone, and even neutral ships within it were to be targets. The sea was even more dangerous because both sides quickly laid mines to prevent surprise raids. An early victim of the mines was LT 760 *Ivy* (a sailing trawler, built 1898 by Chambers and Colby and depicted here in the centre). On 9th December 1914, she left Lowestoft Harbour. Her skipper, William Henry Hills, knew how to avoid the sandbanks, and the weather had not been too bad, so it was strange when she did not return. At an inquiry, held by the Collector of Customs, Samuel Burwood, the skipper of the smack *Pet*, said that he had seen the *Ivy* on 17th December 1914, heading for home. However, she had to wait out at sea overnight, as the regulations did not permit fishing boats to enter the harbour in the darkness. The verdict was that she hit a mine. All hands were lost. The crew are commemorated on the war memorial outside Trinity House London. Also in this picture is LT 455 *Young Percy* (built 1905, Brixham, depicted second from the left). On 28th July 1915, she was stopped by UB 13, commanded by Walter Gustav Becker, 30 miles E by N of Lowestoft and sunk by a time bomb. UB 13's career was cut short when she was caught in a mine net on 24th April 1916, and destroyed with the loss of all the crew.

Much of the North Sea was mined posing a danger to naval and fishing vessels alike. This depicts LT 420 *Roser* (converter-trawler and drifter – built 1884 by S C Allerton), and LT 635 *Chrysolite* trawler (built by Reynolds in 1905 and owned by AE Dexter). On 4th July 1917 she was sunk by a mine 4 miles North of the Haisborough Light Vessel. All of the five crew drowned.

To deal with the problem of mines, smacks were tasked with minesweeping –which involved the dangerous role of locating German mines, without actually running into them, and shooting them with rifle fire. This shows a mine being exploded.

Due to the attacks on fishing vessels, the Royal Navy developed "Q-ships" as decoys to trap and destroy the enemy submarines. These were ordinary merchant ships or fishing boats, covertly armed with concealed guns. When a U-boat appeared, a 'panic party' would ostensibly abandon ship, while a hidden gun crew lay in wait for the U-boat to come closer. Then they would open fire. A good number of local boats were recruited as Q-ships. LT 1095 *Breadwinner* (1907-1942) was a sail trawler built in 1907 by Sanderson. In WW1 she was a Q Ship, alias S 7 *Seagull*, and armed with a 3 pounder gun, from February 1917 to 11th November 1918. She survived the war, and operated through the 1920s and 1930s as a fishing boat. However she fared less well in the Second World War, being bomb damaged on 14 May 1943 and then

broken up. These Q ships had some notable successes, such as on 15th Aug 1915 when the armed smack *Inverlyon* LT 687 under skipper Tom Phillips and Navy Gunner Ernest Jehan (from HMS *Dryad*) sank U-boat 4, commanded by Oblt Karl Gross, which had only the previous day sunk LT 1010 *Bona Fide*, its fourth victim that year. Having surfaced to attack the smack, the U-boat observed the fishing boat crew lounging about and ordered them to abandon ship. The crew moved about as if obeying, but when the U-boat had practically stopped moving, Jehan gave the order to open fire. The *Inverlyon* hoisted the white ensign, dropped the cover off the 3 pounder gun, and fired straight at the U-boat –Jehan killing the German officer with a shot from his revolver. The shells which hit the conning tower caused devastation and the U-boat soon began to sink. As it did so three of the crew floated free –one of whom was calling for help. Skipper Philips stripped off his boots and jacket and dived in to the rescue (despite the dangerous conditions) –but was not able to reach the German before he sunk. The U-boat was sunk with the loss of all 15 crew. For this action Philipps was awarded the DSM, Jehan the DCS and the crew a bounty.

Many soldiers were billeted in Lowestoft during the war. Also posted to Lowestoft were the 19th Queens Regt (the Officers and men shown here in 1917), which was formed in Tunbridge Wells on 19th June 1915 to carry out coastal defence. Known as the Mutton Lancers (after its lamb and flag cap badge), it moved to Lowestoft almost immediately in July 1917. One of the officers was Captain Arthur Brian Ashby, a barrister in Chambers at 2 Pump Court, Temple, London, who was posted to Lowestoft with the Queen's before going to serve as a Court Martial Officer in France. He was accompanied to Lowestoft by his wife Dame Margery Corby Ashby, a prominent suffragette.

Margery Ashby [1882-1981] in common with many suffragettes came from an advantaged background. As well as speaking at National Union of Women's Suffrage Societies meetings (such as one on 17th April 1916, where she described, with lantern slides, the Scottish Women's Hospital work in France, Russia and Serbia), Margery Ashby became heavily involved in the Red Cross activities in the town, and in particular ministering to the many wounded servicemen, recuperating in Lowestoft hospital. Margery's particular contribution was in raising the spirits of the invalids, in order to speed their recovery, by introducing them to embroidery. These photos were - "Specimens of results her embroidery classes in Lowestoft Hospital 1915-1916". They enjoyed making cushion covers of their regimental badges, the outline of which Ashby often had to draw for them.

The Suffragette movement was active in Lowestoft since the beginning. The non-militant National Union of Women's Suffrage Societies founded by Millicent Fawcett in 1897. They soon opened an office in Kirkley on the corner of London Road South and Wellington Road. They campaigned for the right for women to vote. The change did not come quickly enough for some women; in 1903 the militant Women's Social and Political Union 'the Suffragettes ' was founded by Emmeline Pankhurst. They had an office at the bridge near the harbour. These offices were a useful point of contact for the public, where people could get tickets for meetings, or read the posters put up in the windows. As the great powers were readying themselves for the confrontation that would explode in the First World War, the Suffragettes were increasing the tempo of their own campaigns.

Lowestoft's location made it a target also for direct attack, such as happened on 16th April 1915, when L5 bombed it. A great fire which was ignited by an incendiary bomb falling in Latten's timber yard. Lowestoft was bombarded by some German ships that were hoping to tempt the British fleet to chase them into a minefield. In the early hours of 25th April 1916 German battlecruisers, *Derfflinger, Lutzow, Moltke, Seydlitz* and *Von der Tann*, under Bödicker sailed through the mist to attack the harbour, which then acted as a base for part of the British Fleet. Captain Hans Zenker, of the *Von der Tann* recalled that the reduced visibility made picking out targets difficult, but by using the Empire Hotel as a landmark, the Germans were able to train their guns on the bridge and harbour works, and destroy the shore batteries and cause some damage to the town, before they were chased off by Admiral Tyrwhitt's Harwich Force. This shows some of the serious harm caused to the Esplanade in the bombardment.

Banner House

During the War Banner House guest house was occupied by the military, and 78 soldiers were billeted there when it was struck by a shell during the bombardment – not one of them was injured though. Of course, people went hunting for souvenirs of pieces of shells.

There was pretty indiscriminate damage to many parts of the residential districts of Kirkley, such as this house in Windsor road, almost totally destroyed.

The *Lowestoft Journal* recorded that at 4am people were awakened by a terrific boom followed by successive deafening explosions. Shells crashed into the town, or flew screaming overhead and tiles, masonry and bits of metal shrapnel were flying in all directions. The firing went on for 20 minutes, and then went on at sea.

The whole rhythm of life changed in Lowestoft during the war. Brooke Marine was on the north side of Lake Lothing, just beyond the boats. It was opened there in 1911 but during the war it was converted into a munitions factory, and staffed largely by women. Miss E Avery recalled her time working there: "Our job was to make the brass nose cones and very hard work it was. We each had a die in which we placed the brass caps and then proceeded to make the screw end. It was tough going, small bits of brass seemed to be a target for my eyes and I was for ever at the first aid post, having bits extracted.

Eighteen Pakefield men died serving in the Navy or the Royal Navy Reserve. Twenty two died in the Army. The men commemorated perished all across the theatre of war -from the Dardanelles, to Jutland. Four died in the Battle of the Somme, and many of the naval casualties were on armed trawlers and drifters, which fell victim to mines. The Memorial was unveiled on 7th May 1921 by the Dean of Norwich, in front of a gathering of many hundreds of local people.

The end of the war brought no respite from the erosion for Pakefield, as shown by this 1924 photo of houses in the Avenue, Pakefield, facing destruction. In April 1929, *The Times* reported that 'roads that once led to some definite destination now run to the cliff edge. At low tide masses of masonry, old iron and the general equipment of shops and houses lie scattered on the foreshore. Buried somewhere in the sand here is a village green. In 30 years 90 houses have collapsed with the ground on which they stood, and have been pounded by the waves until they have become part of the ocean bed. The action of the sea is slow and persistent. It saps away the base of the cliff until the upper strata and whatever may be standing on it, having become thoroughly undermined, collapse into the water. In the last two years the sea has advanced 80 foot. In one day in January it took a bite of 18 feet......The plight of the fishermen is deplorable. Most of them own their houses and stay in them until the last possible moment. Then a wall cracks, a side falls, and the house is engulfed."

1925. The last of The Avenue being demolished.

1920s view towards Beach St, taken from end of Pakefield Street You can see Beach Street Tea Room In 1925 Lowestoft Corporation needed to replace the groyne at the end of Pakefield Street. Pakefield Council implored them not to make the replacement any longer, lest it exacerbate the scour further. In 1929, the Corporation drew up plans to extend the groynes further south at a cost of about £7,500. In 1930, Lowestoft Corporation finally proposed a scheme to share the cost of protecting the Pakefield cliffs. It proposed a low re-enforced concrete revetment, 11 groynes 300 feet apart and 200 feet long. It would run all the way to Arbour Lane at a cost of £8.600, to be shared between the Corporation, the Rural District Council, the County Council and Pakefield Council. The Pakefield contribution would amount to £60 per year for 15 years. In March 1930, Messrs Lewis and Lewis Engineers of 15 Victoria St, Westminster were engaged to advise on the scheme, and in June 1930 Lowestoft Corporation purchased the Manorial rights to the Pakefield Foreshore for £250. However it would be several years until the work began to have any impact on the erosion.

Written on the back of the above Beach Street cottage postcard:-

A Tale of a Gale [Pakefield 1933]
At number one in Beach Street
Bill Manning used to live
By the sea, it was a treat
No other house could give.

But one dark stormy winters night
The sea came roaring in.
All in Beach Street got a fright
That gale made such a din.

One by one the houses fell
Smashed on the cobbled shore.
And that is all there is to tell
Of a street that is no more."

From Verse of Worse by Walter Page

Throughout the 1930s erosion continued. On 4th May 1933, the *Manchester Guardian* recorded that four children were buried by a fall of cliff at Pakefield, when they were playing on the beach. The children, Ivy and Thora Thurling, Ida Constance and Vera Coates, all of Coronation Terrace, Pakefield, and aged between 8 and 13, were digging in the sand, when the 40 foot cliff cracked and buried them all. They were saved without injury through the prompt action of 13 year old Ronald Haylock, who pulled one of the children out, and called for help to some men who were chatting at the top of the cliff. Two of the children were found clasped in each other's arms, but well. The last to be dug out was Ivy Thurling, who was taken to hospital suffering from partial suffocation and severe shock.

This photograph, taken in 1926, shows the tea room at the end of Beach Street, run by Mrs Crips. Its days, too, were numbered, but she had a good idea. She wrote to the council, in 1929, offering to sell her land to them to enable them to build a sea defence. The council took their time, then several years later, in 1934 they made this decision , - "The offer of Mrs Crips to sell to the corporation a piece of land having frontage of 60 foot to Pakefield Street for a sum of £25 plus legal costs be accepted."

She was just in time, for in January 1934 the new moon and high tides caused further erosion., and a newspaper reported that "Mrs A Crips, who has resided at the Cabin tea rooms for the past 14 years, is now compelled to leave owing to the encroachment of the sea. The café, which now stands on the very edge of the cliff, may at any moment fall into the sea." She served her last cup of tea in 1934 and soon after that the sea took it all.

Jolly Sailors, Pakefield

Beyond the Jolly Sailors public house was Mr Colby's tea room.

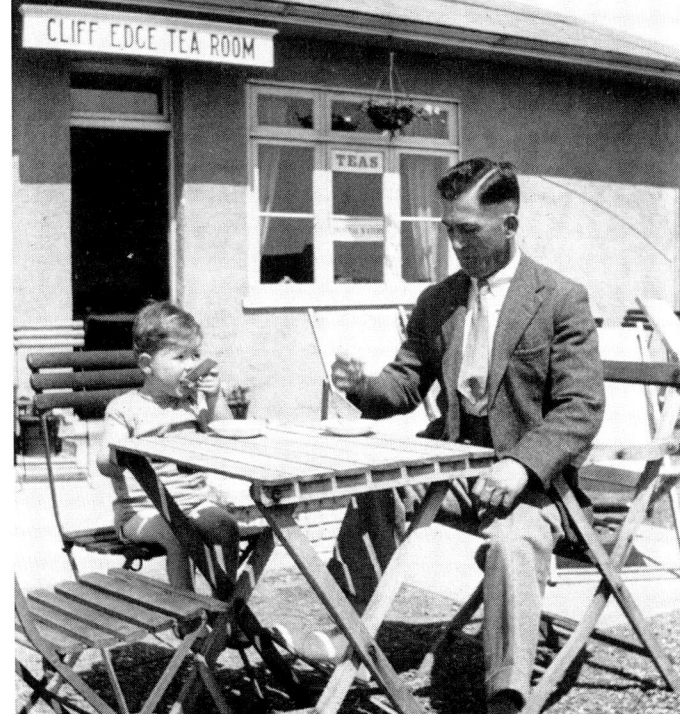

Walter Freeman and little Malcolm, his four year old son, are enjoying ice cream there.

The council meeting minutes record, "That the offer of Mr T Colby to convey to the corporation a piece of land on the Pakefield cliff, be accepted with thanks." Also in 1934 the Borough of Lowestoft Council resolved – "That the council do accept a conveyance from Mr T Colby of land on the east side of Pakefield Road, next to land conveyed from him to the corporation on 17 May 1927, and also the strip of land on the west side of Pakefield Road forming part of Mr Colby's Tea Gardens having frontage of 14 feet and running to the point at the south east corner of the Jolly Sailors Inn, subject to Town Clerks terms and conditions."

1930s, There were previously four garret windows here, in Cliff Road, but the end house has already been demolished. The concrete in the front is the remains of the sea wall built by Mr Davies of the Bungalow long before.

1937, Only houses in Cliff Road remaining. By this time the cliff edge was coming perilously close to Pakefield Church

The storms continued to tear into the Pakefield cliffs. In May 1934 the £49,180 scheme for a continuous promenade from the Claremont Pier to Pakefield began, overseen by Borough Surveyor Sydney W Mobbs. It would be a mass concrete wall at the foot of the cliffs, that would stop the cliffs eroding for good, and halt the damage that Mr Mobbs considered was definitely being caused by the groyne at the end of Pakefield Street. Sydney Mobbs, who died 14 March 1975 at "Windrush" Romany Road, Oulton Broad, was very experienced in constructing sea defences, as Lowestoft had by this time probably the largest sea defence plant in the country, and had carried out all its own work over the preceding 15 years, including the £152,000 North Beach scheme. Indeed he had pioneered the " Lowestoft " system of concrete building, in which flanged blocks are used for two faces of the wall, the flange being continuous on the bottom edge or bed of the block, the block being L-shape in section. The blocks for outside are made of ballast concrete and for the inside of clinker concrete. The flanges of the blocks butt together on the bottom edge and form a continuous trough, which is filled with weak concrete. This picture shows the progress as at December 1934. Much of the work had been carried out by local unemployed people. The work had to progress quickly when conditions permitted, since it could only be carried out when tides were favourable.

In February 1938, there were the worst sea and tide together experienced since 1897. The last, now unoccupied, house in what was formerly Cliff Rd. (number 13), fell into the sea in the moonlight, as people gathered round to watch. In the previous week, it had been possible to cycle in front of the property. Inhabitants of two houses in Pakefield Street, moved bedroom furniture in readiness for a hasty retreat, their ten children slept elsewhere. Gas and water escaped from the snapped pipes when the unoccupied house crashed, it was joined to two others in a block of three. Workmen were called to plug the pipes. The other two houses are occupied. Mr S. Turner of 15 Pakefield Street was in his garden looking over the wall at the sea, when he felt the wall move. As he jumped back so the wall and the place where he had been standing fell into the sea. By next day his back door was only 10 feet from the cliff edge. Some of the worst falls were opposite Pakefield Church, which was fast approaching the edge.

By the close of the 1930s, the coastline had begun to stabilise, and is recognisably the Pakefield cliff we know today. Here we see the Jolly Sailors in the centre on the cliff, flea and bug row has been demolished, and the jumble of dwellings –all that is left of Beach Street and the Cliff, teetering on the brink. Wilson Road has not yet been cut through to Pakefield Street, and the useless revetment remains on the right.

St Luke's Hospital had been a TB hospital since the 1920s, but in June 1940 the whole area in which it stood was scheduled for evacuation, because it was a very prominent building. The patients and equipment – x-ray machines, lino and blackout curtains, were all transferred to other hospitals, in Ascot, Carshalton, London and Northamptonshire. The last patient left on 22nd June 1940. From 18th September 1940, the military authorities requisitioned the ground floor of the hospital to store furniture. On 12th May 1943, an air raid that killed 33 in Lowestoft also caused damage to St. Luke's, when three bombs fell on the foreshore, and cannon shells struck the building. About 2,000 square feet of window glass was destroyed, with damage also to ceilings, roofs, brickwork and woodwork. After this raid, a barrage balloon was flown between St. Luke's and the Grand, one of twelve that were launched above Lowestoft after this raid to deter further attacks. In 1942, St. Luke's became a training school for Royal Naval Patrol Service engineers and stokers –and had two ships engines installed in the basement for them to practice on. The navy remained in St. Luke's until July 1946, by which time it was so damaged that it was considered uneconomical to restore the building to hospital use, so that in January 1947 the Asylum Board decided to close the hospital permanently.

Given all the erosion along the coast, a safer investment than houses was the development of holiday camps and caravan parks. Around 1930, Howard Barrett, who had been born in 1884 in Edmonton, came to Lowestoft to manage the Grand Hotel. He moved in to Pakefield Hall Farm, which had been built in 1849 next to the moated site where an Elizabethan mansion had stood, and which was the ancient settlement of Rodenhall. Seeing the potential of the seaside location, close proximity to Lowestoft and acres of fields, he decided to open a holiday camp. In the 1930s, the camp consisted of 150 acres, and included bowling greens, putting greens, tennis courts and dancing. It also offered spacious dining and dance halls and a fully equipped gymnasium.

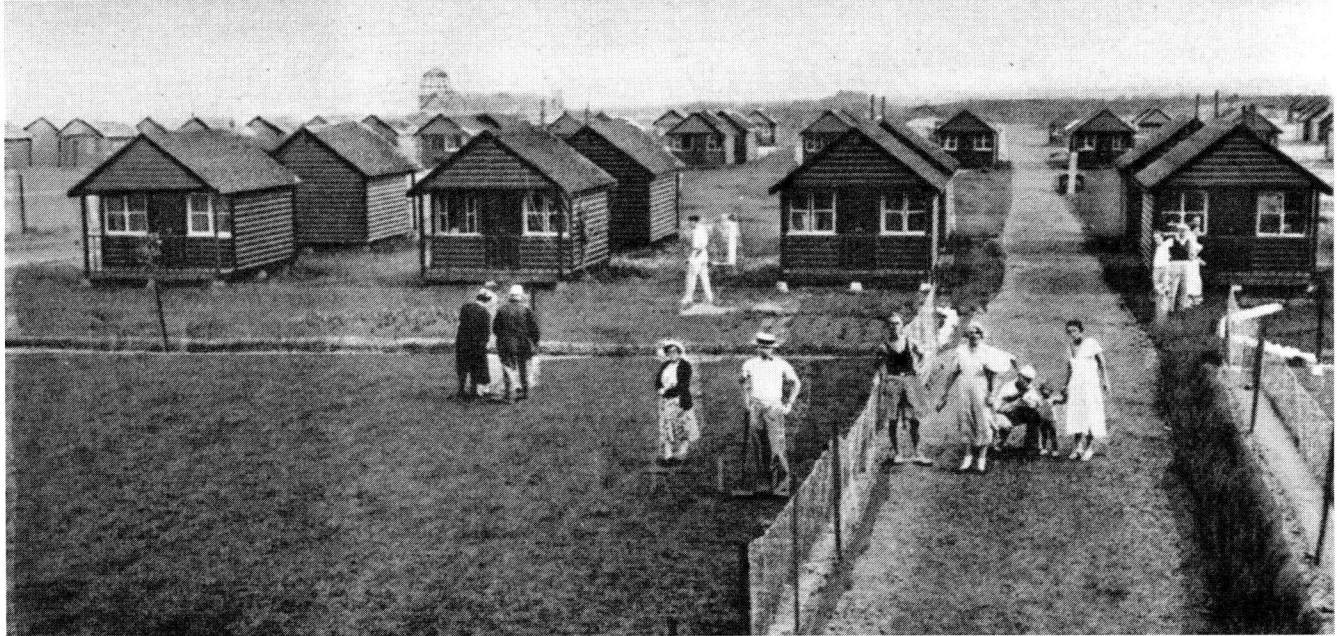

Pakefield Hall Holiday Camp seems to have been based on a military ethos, with tents and huts in straight rows, but unlike the hotels developed for the wealthy, the caravan sites and holiday camp have survived to today. One attraction that was advertised was the possibility to visit the Pakefield Lighthouse, which stands next to the Ravine, described as 'one of the most picturesque spots on the East Coast'.

In 1936 Pakefield Hall Holiday Camp was advertised as "A Bright Breezy and Bracing Holiday," with self-contained bungalows having been recently erected to accommodate 1 to 6 persons, and accommodation made to house 850 visitors, including those under canvas.

However, in the late 1930s as the clouds of war were gathering, Pakefield Hall Holiday Camp was used to house Jewish children refugees brought to the UK as part of the Kindertransport project, while they waited to be relocated in foster homes or hostels. There were 550 children housed in Pakefield, until the extreme winter caused them to be evacuated to a hostel in Norwich. While at the camp, they were taught English customs and manners.

In May 1940 Pakefield Holiday Camp was taken over by Royal Navy personnel, and turned into a fort. In July 1940 the fort was taken over by the Royal Artillery and 326 Battery manned two 6 inch guns sited on the cliff edge. On the beach to the left of the guns was a pill box, and the line in the sand near the edge of the picture is a minefield. Just out of the picture to the left is the lighthouse, which housed a Royal Observer Corps post. On 20th August 1940 they were attacked by three Dornier Flying Pencils, which did not cause much damage, but injured some civilians. But on 4th December 1940 four bombs, were dropped from a lone raider. They damaged the camp area, and blew up six chalets, the Officers Mess, and the men's Recreation Room. Second Lieutenant Latter was instantly killed by the blast. No other casualties occurred. There were gun emplacements and pillboxes all along this quiet stretch of coast, in order to slow a German invasion, and to protect the important naval command centres based in Lowestoft. South of the holiday camp was a radar station. Most of these defences, having remained in situ for about half a century, are now falling into the sea, as the erosion continues.

The Marlborough Hotel was an Officers Mess. Many years later, in the 1970s, the proprietor Joe Beckett while tracing a gas leak, found a stash from this time under the floor boards of one of the bedrooms. There was a hoard of eggs a letter to a girlfriend that had not been posted and an unexploded mortar shell! An army bomb disposal team disposed of the shell.

The Grand was part of a fort manned by 177 Coast Battery. It also manned the observation posts for the two eight inch guns placed in Kensington Gardens, in emplacements disguised as seafront shelters. This shows the Grand before the observation posts were constructed. Throughout the war, several different military units were billeted here. In 1941, the Kings Own Scottish Borderers had their Company dining hall here, and from August 1942, the Independent Czechoslovak Brigade had their headquarters there, while they co-ordinated defence of the coast (including issuing permits for Pakefield fishermen to launch their boats from the beach).

Every family in Pakefield and Kirkley felt the impact of the war. Glen Manna, the home of James Campbell (in the centre of this group posing in the gardens of the house), became a supposed refuge for his daughter Amy Freeman and her children John and Elizabeth, who came here in April 1941 to escape the London bombing. However it turned out that the bombing of Lowestoft was almost as bad. From left to right is Amy holding Elizabeth (one of the authors), Amy's sister Edna, her father James Campbell, and her sister Nora, in the front on the right is John Freeman, and in the centre is Amy's brother Bill Campbell who spent most of the war out in Ceylon. James Campbell was a fish merchant who employed Scottish girls to gut and pack fish for export. His fishing business suffered greatly during the war, both because so little fishing could be done safely, but also because many of his customers had been overseas – for example in Poland.

Amy Freeman was staying at Glen Manna on 21st April 1941, the night that Pakefield Church was bombed. She described the bombing in her letters to her husband Walter, whose job was to deliver petrol to RAF airfields. She wrote to her husband: "what a night we had last night, bombs all around us, incendiary and explosive. Nora put one out on the lawn, and Pa one in the bush near the rockery. Three went through the roof of the Tramway Hotel, and some over the road in front of Bartell's shop and one right next to the wall by the lawn. The big ones rocked the cellar, one fell by Bill's allotment and made a crater 45 feet across, and then one down Carlton Road near the golf links, one in Kirkley cemetery and the Venlaw and St. Luke's and Pakefield Church is burnt out. I feel as though I should like to live in a house all by itself in the middle of the country instead of a town." In this picture we can see the firemen trying to put out the flames. The first man up the ladder is the father of Alan Palmer, who ran Thompson's Shoe Shop, which was also bombed.

Pakefield Church was left as a burnt out shell. Describing the raids, Amy Freeman wrote in May 1941, "we have had raids three nights running and the warning has gone again just now. My bed has been moved down into the cellar as last night we kept getting up, the raids here are really awful. I think I shall go back to Ilford and get the Town Hall to evacuate us to Aberdare, or wherever they send the school children. Sunday we went for a walk along Kessingland Road, and no sooner had we got as far as the lane down to Bill's allotment then away went the warning and over came two planes and back home we had to go." At this point the letter was interrupted, and she continued the next day, "I have started again as we had to go down the cellar and I was there for the night, what a life, the baby [Elizabeth] has been fretful again this afternoon. I think it is the effect of the raids on the milk." She continued "we have had another raid this dinner time, it just seems all raids here.

They bombed the North end along by Hollingsworth's House. The London Road is roped off from Surrey St to Old Nelson St and Wooly's is burnt out –this happened Sunday Night. I dread the nights coming here somehow." A few days later she described a further raid –"in the evening we had another raid and a sailor was blown out of his bedroom and his head blown off in the house on Denmark Road at the corner of their turning."

While the church lay in ruins, the erosion continued. In 1943 there were high tides, and a heavy swell scoured large areas of cliffs, reaching the ancient churchyard: now a corner of the churchyard, with its enclosing wall, tumbled down to the beach. This picture shows in detail the part of the graveyard that was to fall into the sea, together with some large fenced graves. To the left, are the houses which Rev Hunt purchased to augment the graveyard in the 1930s. It is likely their owners were relieved to get something for them!

The burning of Pakefield Church, and the likely loss to erosion, was a blow for Rev. Stather Hunt (rector 1927-1953). He had restored the church before the Second World War only to see it destroyed by fire in the air raid of 1941. With the end of the war, he set about restoring the church, and his personal devotion and example inspired the parish to such endeavour that the church was rebuilt and rededicated on 29th January 1950 by the Bishop of Norwich.

The landowners of the Cliftonville Estate had learned their lesson. No more ambitious or grandiose building schemes. Where Mr Davies dreamt of marine villas, shops and hotels, and where before the war, lads used to go to spy on courting couples, J Colby set up the Cliftonville Caravan site off Arbour Lane on Pakefield cliff top. In August 1952 the Journal mentioned that he had left the bushes to screen the caravans from one another, and positioned them so that the camp did not have the usual depressingly regimental sets of straight lines.

In about 1959, Cresta Caravan site followed suit, being established right on the cliff edge, just near the 16 acre site. It was run by Mr Miney. The holiday camp, too, released now by the military was back in action, rebranded as New Pakefield Holiday Camp. Then in 1958 Sir Fred Pontin took it over, and enlarged it to accommodate around 1,400 holidaymakers.

The 1950s brought stability and new opportunities for the people of Pakefield. The sea wall had finally stopped the erosion, the ruined houses could be torn down and replaced, and new roads made. The sea wall, built by Sydney Mobbs, the Lowestoft Borough Surveyor, despite the scare of 1943, has saved Pakefield from destruction, and preserved the cliffs until today. The groynes cast into the sea have allowed the beach to build up, so that it now nearly covers the promenade. Now, the defences to the left of the picture are buried under a couple of metres of shingle.

The sea can still show its wild strength. In 1953, a good part of Lowestoft was flooded, and as can be seen here, 1953 storms the Kirkley promenade was damaged.